T0057354

# The Essential
# DEHYDRATOR

# The Essential
# DEHYDRATOR

From Dried Mushroom Risotto to Grilled Tuna with Papaya Chutney,
**More Than 100 Recipes Bursting with Fresh Flavor**

SUSAN PALMQUIST and JILL HOUK

Avon, Massachusetts

Copyright © 2013 by Susan Palmquist and Jill Houk.
All rights reserved.
This book, or parts thereof, may not be reproduced in any form without permission from the publisher;
exceptions are made for brief excerpts used in published reviews.

Published by
Adams Media, a division of F+W Media, Inc.
57 Littlefield Street, Avon, MA 02322. U.S.A.
*www.adamsmedia.com*

ISBN 10: 1-4405-6002-1
ISBN 13: 978-1-4405-6002-6
eISBN 10: 1-4405-6003-X
eISBN 13: 978-1-4405-6003-3

Printed in the United States of America.

10   9   8   7   6   5   4   3   2   1

Always follow safety and commonsense cooking protocol while using kitchen utensils, operating ovens and stoves, and handling uncooked food. If children are assisting in the preparation of any recipe, they should always be supervised by an adult.

Many of the designations used by manufacturers and sellers to distinguish their product are claimed as trademarks. Where those designations appear in this book and F+W Media was aware of a trademark claim, the designations have been printed with initial capital letters.

Photos courtesy of Angela Garbot.

*This book is available at quantity discounts for bulk purchases.*
*For information, please call 1-800-289-0963.*

## DEDICATION

To my mother, Donna Yule, who taught me to cook at the age of ten and encouraged me to become a professional chef.

—Jill Houk

# ACKNOWLEDGMENTS

## From Susan Palmquist

As always I'd like to thank my late parents for always believing in me as a writer . . . and for telling everyone what a great cook I am. Life may have gotten in the way of me opening the restaurant I dreamed about owning, but writing about food is the next best thing.

Thanks also to Mrs. Jones, my former domestic science teacher for teaching me everything I know about cooking and turning me into an avid cook and foodie (despite my early protests about wanting to transfer to the boys' woodworking class).

To my writing students, from whom I learn as much as they do from me.

To Flynn, my constant writing companion.

To Jeff for oftentimes coming home to see our kitchen housing an assortment of dirty pots, pans, and general disarray as I tested recipes for this book. And for being the taste-test guinea pig.

## From Jill Houk

Many thanks to Nicole and Jeff Joslyn and to Alexi Mandolini for lending me their dehydrators for recipe development and testing. To Anne Guillemette for expanding my ideas of all a dehydrator could do. Thanks to Angela Garbot for her photography skills and endless laughs during our food photo shoots. Also thanks to Carrie Schloss for her food styling expertise and recipe testing.

And, finally, thanks to my husband, Scott, and my son, Sam, for willingly eating and giving feedback on the recipes.

# Contents

## CHAPTER 5: FRUITS  63

## CHAPTER 6: MEATS AND FISH  93

## CHAPTER 7: HERBS AND DAIRY  105

## Part III: Prepare Delectable Recipes Using Your Dried Food  125

# Introduction

Welcome to the wonderful world of dehydration. Not only is it one way that food can be preserved for later enjoyment, but it's going to get you thinking about a new way of cooking! You'll find yourself using such things as dried cherries, papaya, and even seafood. Dehydrated food can be stored for a long time, saving you money and shelf space, and it can add new and exciting flavors to your dishes.

Once you begin preserving food this way, it's tough to stop because you see so many possibilities. Before you know it, it's a new hobby. You'll also find that you can use a dehydrator for other things besides drying foods. You can make your own yogurt or use the dehydrator to get homemade bread to rise. How cool is that? You can make homemade granola and energy bars at a fraction of the cost of store-bought ones—plus, you'll know what's in them. And if you're budget-minded, you can dry leftover foods for long-term storage. The possibilities are endless!

## WHAT WILL YOU FIND IN THIS BOOK?

To kick things off, we'll explain how dehydrating works and what to look for when you buy a machine. You'll also learn how to prepare foods for dehydration. Best of all, we'll guide you through the steps needed to rehydrate them so they're ready for eating or using in recipes.

Next, we'll take you through the process of dehydrating vegetables, fruits, meats, fish, herbs, and dairy products. Finally, in the last part of this book, you'll find gourmet recipes: everything from appetizers to main dishes to desserts. These recipes will have you rethinking dried foods. They're for dishes that you can find in some of the top restaurants in the country, yet easy enough for the at-home cook to put together any night of the week.

Okay, roll up your sleeves, turn on the dehydrator, and let's get started!

# PART I

# Learn the Basics

In this section you'll find everything you need to know about dehydrating foods. Even if you've never dried something before or never used a dehydrator, don't worry because by the time you get to the end of this part, you'll be an expert.

# CHAPTER 1

# What Is Dehydration?

Not only have humans been hunting and gathering food since time began; we've also been preserving it. There's nothing new about prolonging the shelf life of the foods we grow or buy. By drying foods we ensure there's always something available in the cupboard that's good and nutritious to eat. If you've never thought about drying foods before, once you discover how fun it is you may never go back to canning or freezing food again.

There's an excellent chance that one of your ancestors used to dry things like fruits and vegetables. In fact, it's the oldest method of preserving food. Early civilizations harnessed the sun and wind to dry berries, roots, and even grasses. Native American tribes and early American settlers dried foods in order to survive both droughts and harsh winters.

Dehydration might sound complicated, but the process is an easy one. Foods have high water content. When you dry food you remove most of this water, which stops the growth of organisms such as yeast, enzymes, and bacteria, all of which lead to spoilage. Fruits and vegetables consist of about 80–95 percent water and meats are 50–75 percent water. Dehydration takes their water content down to around 10 percent while leaving most of the full nutritional value of the food intact. Dehydration also acts as a natural food preservative.

## WHY DEHYDRATE?

But, you may be saying, what about canning? What about freezing? What's wrong with these methods of preservation? Here are some reasons why many people choose drying over the other methods of food preservation.

- *Less time and skill required.* If you've ever tried canning and given up because things didn't turn out as planned, take comfort: Dehydrating foods is a lot easier and less time consuming. Even if you've never done it before, dehydrating is a skill you can quickly learn and, indeed, become an expert at. And let's be honest—who really wants to spend time canning foods in the middle of summer when your kitchen already feels as if it's 110°F? Using a dehydrating machine produces very little heat so you won't lose your cool even if it's 90°F outside and you're running the machine all day.

- *Less storage space needed.* The era of living in oversized houses is gone, and these days many of us have moved into smaller homes. Maybe your grown children have moved back with you or your family's had a recent young addition. Either way we need to make the most of the space we have. The last thing we want to do is fill shelves with canned foods or even a chest freezer taking up valuable feet in the basement or garage. Dehydrating shrinks foods down to one-tenth of their original size, so a pound of carrots can easily fit into a small jar. If you have a small kitchen or limited storage space, dehydration is for you.

- *Capture flavor when it's at its freshest.* One of the best things about summer is the abundance and variety of produce. However, a major drawback is when it's hot and humid the food spoils quickly and you can only eat so much of it. Dehydrating allows you to have the best of both worlds.

- *Make preservation pay off.* We all love to eat something tasty and sweet in between meals. When you dehydrate fruits, their flavors not only become more concentrated but they get sweeter and therefore make the ideal snack for both kids and adults.

- *Derive maximum nutrition.* You've heard it over and over again; turn on the TV and there's some nutritionist telling us to eat five servings of fruits and vegetables a day. We know it makes sense but sometimes it's not easy to squeeze them in. You can solve the problem by having some dried fruits to throw on your breakfast cereal or in that brown-bag lunch. Drying foods as soon as you bring them home seals in all their flavors, colors, and essential nutrients. Many people think it's as good as eating the food fresh.

- *Enjoy preservative-free food.* If you're a label detective, you'll know that even a bag of apricots can contain ingredients that warrant an advanced degree in chemistry to decipher. Dry your own foods and you'll know what's in them every time.

- *Save money.* Watching your food budget? With the continual increase in prices at the supermarket, who isn't worried about inflation and how to feed your family? You'll be a cool penny-pincher when you become an avid dehydrator. When food is abundant, it's at its lowest price and you can snag a bargain. It's a great time to preserve and store all types of foods for later use when prices go higher.

- *Save money on preserving and equipment.* Using an electric dehydrator will cost you half as much as canning, and almost seven times less than freezing. And just think of the money you'll save because you no longer need jars and a supply of new lids every year.
- *Preserve your garden.* Perhaps you're one of the many people who like to grow vegetables in their backyard. Now you'll have no reason to toss out that pile of zucchini or tub of tomatoes. Drying them is an easy and cost-effective way to keep them for future meals. And it's not just an overabundance of fresh produce you can dry. If you open a can of tomato paste and only need a tablespoon, place the remaining amount in the dehydrator and save it for another recipe.
- *Create emergency food supplies.* Turn to the Weather Channel and you're likely to hear that we're heading toward a record season for something or other. If you live in a hurricane- or tornado-prone area, you know how important it is to have a supply of food should the power or water supply be affected by a storm. Dried foods are light, space-efficient, and easy to take with you should the worst-case scenario happen and you're forced to flee your home.
- *Stock up on camping equipment.* One of the pleasures of sitting around a campfire is eating foods you've brought with you. However, who wants to be weighed down along a trail with cans of beans and soup? Dehydration makes food lightweight and the most practical take-along meal that can fit into any backpack.

Hopefully we've now convinced you how great dehydrating is, so let's move on to some of the tools of the trade. There's more good news there because unlike canning, you'll need fewer tools.

# CHAPTER 2
# Methods of Dehydration

Later in this chapter we'll show you some natural methods of dehydrating, using the sun and wind. But for now, let's discuss dehydrating machines. Buying a dehydrator to successfully dry foods may not be essential for the dedicated dehydrator, but let's just say once you've used one you won't want to ever be without it.

Basically these machines mimic nature. They replace the sun with a heating element to dry the food and use a fan to create wind to suck out all its moisture. Fruits and vegetables need to be dried at around 115°F–120°F, and dehydrators are efficient at getting that temperature just right.

Most dehydrating machines are either round or square. Some are designed to allow you to add more trays if you want. Some trays are made of fine mesh, while others have larger gaps/slats between them which often means you need to cover them with plastic wrap or parchment paper to prevent foods from slipping through to the lower levels as the food dries and shrinks. And yes, ones with larger mesh racks are often harder to clean than ones with finer mesh.

Google "dehydrators" and you'll find lots of brands and models to choose from. They range from well-known brands such as Excalibur, Nesco, and American Harvest to smaller, lesser-known companies. American Harvest has the largest line of dehydrators in this country; they offer eleven different models. With so much choice, what should you look for?

## Be a Shrewd Buyer

There are many factors you should consider while you're shopping for a dehydrator. You're going to be using this machine for many years so it's best to take your time, ask questions, and even check with friends who own one to see what they like and dislike about their make and model. Should the one you bought not live up to your expectations, many manufacturers have a thirty-day money-back guarantee.

The higher-wattage machines often cost more but get the job done much faster. Don't worry about the cost of running these machines. It can be scary to think that a dehydrator must be turned on and using electricity for up to eighteen hours, but a 750-watt machine costs, on average, about eight cents an hour to operate.

While shopping for a dehydrator, you'll quickly notice the price range. Some machines cost as little as $59 while others are close to $300. If you're not sure if drying foods is for you or you just want to dry tomatoes once in a while, a machine at the lower end of the range may be all you need. However, if this is something you want to do for years to come or you're planning to dehydrate lots of food every week, paying more for a machine makes sense. The more money you invest, the more features you'll get.

Most machines are available for purchase online either through a specialty site or the manufacturer's own website. Some models can be found in stores such as Bed, Bath & Beyond or through third-party vendors. Even a perusal of Amazon will show you a range of models and prices. A couple of the manufacturers have factory outlets where you can pick up a machine at discount. And don't overlook garage sales and thrift stores. Some people buy a machine, let it sit for a while, and then decide it's not for them. That's good news for you because such machines, virtually unused, usually sell at a huge discount.

### Questions to Ask

When buying a dehydrator, first ask yourself how much food you'll be drying. If you're just starting out, a smaller model with a couple of trays may be perfect for you. However, if you know you've got a whole vegetable garden to preserve, opt for a model with eight or nine trays and/or one to which more trays can be added as needed.

Also check where the fan is located. Cheaper models usually feature a bottom-based fan, which can be a problem when juices from meats or bits of food shrink (as they dry) and drop down into, or near it. This often means more cleanup for you.

Most models have fans, but higher-priced models locate them on the side of the machine, which forces the air horizontally across the foods instead of vertically. Not only does this prevent the falling foods from sliding into the fan, but flavors and odors are less likely to blend together.

Cheaper models usually have only one temperature and fan speed so you can't vary it for individual recipes or to speed up the drying process. Higher-end models often have timers so if you want to dry food during the night and don't want to get up at two in the morning to check that all is well, you can set the machine to turn itself off.

Don't forget to look for a UL-approved model—one with at least a one-year warranty and an enclosed heating element and fan. Last but not least, purchase a model with a double-wall construction that fits on your kitchen countertop (or wherever else you're going to put it).

Whatever model you decide to buy, remember that overall success depends upon the type of food you're drying, the amount, and the food's water content. Foods with more water require a longer drying time. Thickness of food plays a major factor in the dehydrating process, as does surrounding relative humidity. For example, drying foods in Florida in August is going to produce different results than drying them in Arizona that same month.

Another variable is sugar content. The higher the sugar content of a food, the longer it takes to dry. One great thing about the higher-end dehydrator models is they tend to dry all foods faster and more efficiently than the cheaper models, without the need to rotate foods and trays. And the faster foods dry, the more vitamin content they retain.

## OTHER EQUIPMENT

Besides a dehydrator machine there are a few other things that can help you prepare foods and ensure success. The best news is they won't break the bank.

Sharp knives mean quicker work for you and less bruising for the produce. A sharp, durable knife that can be easily re-sharpened is the prime tool for getting foods ready for the dehydrator. Look for an eight- to twelve-inch stainless steel chef's knife. Not only can stainless steel be sharpened, but it also won't brown the food, which will look more appetizing when it's dried.

Lots of apples to peel and core? Invest in an apple peeler, which does everything . . . peels, cores, and slices. The cost is less than $30 and it's a nice gadget for the avid food dehydrator.

To make the pre-preparation stage less of a chore you'll need a cutting board. This should be wooden or soft plastic so it doesn't dull the knife. It's also a good idea to invest in a honing tool or sharpening steel. We recommend washing and honing your knife after you've cut each vegetable.

Another nice addition to your dehydrator kitchen is a food processor. Many have discs that are ideal for slicing fruits and vegetables. As a food processor will create even-sized pieces, it's perfect for dehydrating preparation. A favorite tool of chefs, although expensive, is a mandoline, which also produces consistent slices. You can adjust the thickness of the cut for the different foods you prepare. (Sadly, a really good mandoline can cost you $300, and cheap ones probably aren't worth the investment.) An egg slicer is perfect for soft foods like mushrooms and strawberries, but unfortunately though it's budget friendly, its blades can't be adjusted or sharpened.

### Storage

Once foods have been dehydrated you'll need something to store them in so they last longer. This can be as simple as a plastic storage bag or even one of the Foodsaver machines that suck out all the air and seal the bag or container. Most people use everyday jars and containers.

## DEHYDRATING WITHOUT A DEHYDRATOR

If a dehydrator isn't in your budget right now or you just want to dry things like toma-toes to use in recipes and you don't think it's worth your while to purchase a machine, here are some other ways you can dehydrate.

### Solar Dehydrating

Using the sun's heat and the wind to move air across food is the cheapest way to dry it. Fruits are best because they have high sugar and acid content, whereas the opposite is true of vegetables and meats, so we don't recommend solar drying for them.

The process is simple—set the food outside to sit in the sun a few days where it dries and has its water content greatly reduced.

You'll need two or three consecutive days of high temperatures in the mid-nineties accompanied by low humidity. A brisk wind is also a must. Most people use wooden trays or slates and place the food directly onto them. Netting or cheesecloth placed over the trays is also a good idea to stop bugs and birds from eating the food while it's drying. It's best to bring the food indoors at night, and a definite must if rain is in the forecast.

If you're the adventurous type you can make or buy an actual solar dryer that reflects the sun's heat. Besides a heat source, you'll need a ventilation system, which increases air flow. The ideal place to live for solar dehydrating is an area that's not so hot and doesn't have high humidity.

For instructions to build your own solar dryer, check out this website: *www.solarfooddryer.com*

### Oven Dehydrating

If you don't want to invest in a machine or don't live in an area with optimum weather conditions for outdoor dehydrating, there's a device you can use—one that we all have sitting in our kitchens. It's called an oven. It's a little more time consuming and gives less predictable results than a dehydrator, but don't let that stop you.

Oven drying is similar to using a dehydrator except most ovens don't adjust to as low a temperature as do dehydrators. The lowest setting for most ovens is 180°F or 200°F. If you dehydrate using an oven, remember that the air is warmest closest to its heating element and therefore that's a good spot to place the food. The best foods to dry using this method are tomatoes, herbs, kale, apricots, grapes, and strawberries.

To oven dehydrate, slice and dip the food in the same substances, such as lemon juice, as if you were using a dehydrator; then lay it flat on a cookie sheet. Place a small electric fan near the oven to get the air moving around.

If you're using a gas oven leave the door open eight inches. Most people find that the warmth from the pilot light is all the dehydrating process needs so sometimes there's no need to turn the oven on. With an electric oven you need to open the door just two inches. On both ovens, rotate the trays every thirty minutes during the whole cooking time and be sure to turn the food over for even drying. Halfway through the drying process should be ideal. The amount of time you need to dry will vary depending on the heat and humidity in the oven, a factor you can't always vary. And there's no major difference in time and method between a gas and electric oven.

### Hang-Drying

There's one more way to dry foods and it's the easiest and cheapest: hang-dry them. Herbs dry very well by this method. Just pull bunches of them from your garden or buy them at the store. Shake off the dirt, give them a good rinse, and shake them dry . . . a salad spinner is perfect for this. Gather together about three or four stems and tie them with raffia or twine. Hang the herbs root side up, leaf side down. The room in which you hang them should be well ventilated as you don't want a buildup of moisture. After two or three days you can check how they're doing. You can tell when they're ready because they'll be crisp, completely dry, and crumble into a powder when you press them between your fingers. Onions and garlic are great for hang-drying too, and many people braid them together and hang them on a hook.

## PREPARING YOUR FOODS FOR DEHYDRATION

You're almost ready to begin dehydrating your first batch of food. While preserving foods this way is simple, there are a few steps you need to take before you start. If possible, plan on shopping for your produce and dehydrating it on the same day because the foods will be at their freshest. You also have the best chance to lock in flavor, color, and nutrition.

### Time to Be Choosy

Selecting the best foods to dehydrate plays a major role in how well they turn out. Take some time to be picky.

Choose fruits and vegetables that are free of blemishes, any rotten spots, and yes, mold. All are an indication that the produce is past its prime. It's not something you want to eat now or preserve for later. You're looking for produce that is at the peak of its maturity so that you're guaranteed the best color and flavor that will last throughout the drying process.

Speaking of color, as you browse the produce aisles pick items that have the deepest hues. For example, opt for the reddest tomatoes, the greenest broccoli, and the kumquats that are the brightest orange.

Selecting great-looking and -tasting produce isn't for wallflowers. Don't be shy about picking up each item of fruit and vegetable to inspect it and weigh it. You're not looking for the biggest of the bunch, just the heaviest. Heavier produce is more laden with juice and therefore contains more flavor. You don't need scales to tell which is heavier. Like most things in cooking, your hands are perfect instruments for this task. In addition to looking at the grocery supermarket for produce to dry, try your local farmers' markets, roadside stands, or pick-your-own farms. And don't overlook the growing number of CSAs (Community Supported Agriculture). Joining a CSA is the perfect way to not only buy lower-cost produce, it's also the ideal route to get an extra supply for preserving. At the beginning of the year you pay a certain amount of money to a participating farm. In return for this up-front investment you get a share of their crop. Every couple of weeks during their harvest you'll get a box of whatever the farm grows. It could be herbs, flowers, vegetables, or fruit. Everything in a CSA box is always at peak freshness. An added plus is many of the farms taking part in CSAs are certified organic.

If meats are on your list of things to dry, make sure you select lean cuts of meat such as flank steak, top, and sirloin. Game meats (bison, pheasant, etc.) also make excellent jerky, as do turkey and chicken breasts.

How about heading to your local ethnic market or even a mom-and-pop grocery store? Big supermarkets often have less ripe produce because they buy in bulk. Smaller ethnic stores often buy smaller quantities of riper fruits and vegetables. And don't forget fresh fish markets are worth checking out too.

## Clean Your Food

Always clean and dry your food thoroughly. Since dehydration is all about taking out water, try to avoid adding extra moisture during the cleaning process. You don't want to preserve your food with pathogens either, so make sure they're dirt- and soil-free. Remove pits, stems, and peels that can become dry and bitter when dehydrated. (Things such as apple peels can also increase the drying time.) Remove waxed peels as well. Prepare meats by taking out bones and cutting away the fat.

## How to Blanch

As a rule of thumb if a vegetable needs to be blanched before you'd freeze it, it's wise to blanch it before you dry it. Say we want to dehydrate broccoli. By the time we take it off the racks of the dehydrator we want it to be both vibrant in color and taste so we blanch it. It's a little work with a big reward.

Bring a large pot of water to a rolling boil. Drop in the food and cook it for thirty seconds. Remove it from the water and quickly plunge it into a large bowl of ice-cold water to stop it from cooking further. This helps foods stay flavorful and vibrant during the drying process as well as halting enzyme reaction in the food, which stops it from deteriorating during storage.

......................................................................................................................

### What You *Shouldn't* Blanch

One word of caution here. Do *not* blanch mushrooms, strawberries, onions, or sweet bell peppers. These items will absorb too much water during the blanching process and will not dehydrate properly.

......................................................................................................................

Some people also blanch by steaming. You don't need any fancy equipment. Pick up one of the collapsible stainless steamers you see in the aisles of supermarkets for less than $5. Put the vegetables inside and steam them over boiling water for five minutes, then plunge them into a bowl of cold water.

Some vegetables and fruits, such as plums and cherries, have tough skins. It's bad enough eating them when they're fresh but once they're dried, there's a good chance you'll need the dentist's number on speed dial. Here's another case where blanching comes to the rescue. If you don't want to blanch them another alternative is to simply peel them.

Do you ever notice when you're shopping in the produce department that some fruits such as grapes and blueberries, and even some vegetables, have a shiny, wax-like look to them? Not that they can't be dehydrated—they can—but you need to get rid of that look. When you dehydrate food you need its moisture to come to the surface in order for it to escape and evaporate. The moisture can't do that with these waxy layers coating the food.

Bring a pot of water to a boil, place the fruit into it, boil it for thirty to sixty seconds, and then blanch the fruit in very cold water. Some people take a shortcut and use a toothpick or tine of a fork to make tiny piercings on the surface of the fruit, which also allows it to dry out faster. Either method works fine.

····················································································

**Avoid Veggie Garlic Breath**

Dehydrate garlic and onions all by themselves because if you don't other foods will absorb their odor.

····················································································

## Go for Good Looks

As we mentioned earlier, you don't want browned dehydrated foods. We've all seen it happen to foods when we prepare them. Most prone are peaches, bananas, potatoes, apples, and pears. Their high sugar content causes them to oxidize, and it's this oxidization that causes the ugly brown look.

There's an easy solution to make them look pretty again: Dip them in a slightly acidic solution. You can use lemon, orange, or even pineapple juice, all of which add a nice sweetness to the dried foods. For us there's nothing better than dried bananas that have been dipped in orange juice. Some people even use an ascorbic acid solution, which is really just vitamin C and is available at most places where dehydrators and supplies are purchased. Others take a shortcut by putting the lemon juice into a spray bottle and coating them with juice instead of dipping them. Whatever way you prefer, once they're done, shake them dry and then place them straight into the dehydrator.

····················································································

**No Lemon on Green, Please**

Don't try the lemon juice (or anything acidic) on green foods such as broccoli and herbs. The acid in the juice will destroy the chlorophyll (which is what makes the food green) and you'll end up with yucky brownish-gray food.

····················································································

A nice addition to dehydrating fruit is to candy it. Bring a cup of water plus a cup of granulated white sugar to a boil and boil until the mixture is clear, around three or four minutes. Cool it and use it as a dip for the fruits.

All this soaking and dipping might sound like we're adding more moisture to the food when we want to take it out. However, these steps are necessary for the produce to work best. Just remember that all these things add some time to the overall drying period.

Some people buy dehydrators to make fruit leathers, and for these sweet treats the rules change somewhat. You don't have to be so picky; you can use ripe and overripe foods. Cut them into chunks and estimate that two cups of fruit will make a 13" × 15" fruit leather.

Many people are surprised to learn when they start dehydrating food that it's not all about fresh produce. You can use frozen and canned foods too. In fact, because processed fruits and veggies are picked and frozen or canned at the height of ripeness, they can be fresher than fresh produce that's out of season. For frozen produce, defrost it and then press out excess water. The same goes for canned fruits: Just drain, give the food a good rinse, and then let it dry.

## Making Jerky

If you want to make jerkies, preparation is easy. Slice the meat with the grain in long, thin, even strips. It's also best to marinate it in something salty (like teriyaki or soy sauce) for twenty-four hours in the fridge. Make sure all the meat is covered. Partly freezing the meat before you slice it makes it much easier to get thin slices. Aim for ⅛"–¼" thick and 1½" wide by 4"–12" long.

Fish should be washed, dried, and cut into ¼" strips. The best fish for dehydrating include cod, snapper, flounder, sole, halibut, and haddock. Fish with a high oil content shouldn't be dehydrated because its higher fat content makes it more prone to spoilage. Such fish includes trout (both lake and rainbow) and mackerel.

Even if you haven't been picky about cutting foods to the exact same sizes before, now's the time to become a perfectionist. Same-size pieces dry at the same rate and will all be ready at the same time. So cut your food into pieces that are close to equal in size.

One rule of thumb that applies to all foods is that the higher the water content of the food, the larger the piece you'll need. Opt for pieces ⅛"–½" thick.

......................................................................

**Spin the Water Away**

One kitchen item that's really helpful in eliminating water from things like herbs is a salad spinner. You can pick them up cheap at the grocery store.

......................................................................

# CHAPTER 3
# Techniques for Dehydrating and Rehydrating

The major thing that worries most people who are new to dehydrating foods is knowing when the food's ready. Here's an overall picture of what you're aiming for.

### Check Early and Often

Start checking the food at the low end of the suggested drying time. For example, if a recipe suggests 8–12 hours, check after 8 hours and then every half hour after that. Don't forget to turn foods over; one side might be dry but the underside could still have some moisture remaining.

A good way to test for doneness is to actually touch the food. Most people rely on the following four categories to guide them.

1. **Crisp**—When you bend it, the food breaks. This includes apples, bananas, green beans, cabbage, celery, citrus fruits, corn, garlic, leeks, mushrooms, potatoes, radishes, rhubarb, and tomatoes.
2. **Brittle**—If you break the food up, it should look like cake crumbs. This includes asparagus, avocados, beets, strawberries, broccoli, Brussels sprouts, carrots, ginger, onions, parsnips, peas, peppers, zucchini, and herbs.
3. **Leathery**—The food will look shriveled and bend but neither cracks nor breaks. This includes blueberries, cherries, cranberries, dates, eggplant, grapes, pineapples, plums, and strawberries.

4. **Pliable/Soft**—You can bend it but it shouldn't break. This includes apricots, cantaloupe, kiwi, mangoes, nectarines, papayas, peaches, pears, watermelon, meat, poultry, and fish jerky.

Fruit leathers are done when you can remove them from the plastic wrap in large pieces. Fruit leather also congeals nicely and forms a rubbery sheet.

Some people use a hammer to test if vegetables are properly dehydrated. If they shatter when you hit them, they're ready. (Wear goggles for safety, and going outside to do this is always a smart idea.)

Here's another quick trick to test if a food's dry enough. Take some of whatever you're dehydrating and put it into a plastic bag. Close it and wait a couple of minutes. If you can see beads of moisture inside, it's not quite ready.

You want to avoid what's known as case hardening. This occurs when you've set the dehydrator too high and the outside of the food dries out before the moisture has escaped from its middle. If you're using an electric dehydrator, note that foods you place on the outside of the trays always dry first. Sometimes it's a good idea to move them around while they're drying. You'll learn after trying a few batches that the drying time can vary even when you're dehydrating the same food variety you've worked with before. The bottom line is sometimes you can have great success on one try and complete failure on the next. However, that's part of the fun and learning process, so never get discouraged.

---

**How High Is Your Food?**

Altitude can affect drying time as can humidity. As well, drying time will be influenced by how thick you cut the food.

---

It's very tempting, especially when you're new to dehydrating, to test the pieces as soon as you turn off the machine. However, take a few pieces off the dehydrator and let them cool first. Warm food feels soft and therefore is not a true indicator of doneness.

Once you have the foods all properly dehydrated, the next step is to store them to ensure maximum shelf life. Remember that *moisture is public enemy number one*. The air is full of it, which can easily ruin even the most perfectly dehydrated foods. The second important point to remember is that *heat produces moisture*. So always cool food completely before you store it. Even a small amount of heat on the inside of a container can spell disaster for a perfect batch of dried foods.

If you've dehydrated fruits, they need to be conditioned first. This simply means they need ten days to rest before they can be stored. Conditioning equalizes the moisture and reduces the risk of mold. Just pack them loosely in plastic or a glass jar, seal it, and shake it every day for about a week. It's also a good test to check if the food was properly dehydrated. Should you notice moisture forming on the container it means the food hasn't been dried enough.

Don't panic if you over-dehydrate something. We've all done it—thought a food wasn't dried properly and stuck it back on the rack to dry it some more . . . and yes, it came out a little shriveled. But that's okay, because you can add moisture back by letting it stay in the open air for a few hours.

## STORING YOUR DEHYDRATED FOOD

When it comes to containers for storing your dried foods, you don't need anything fancy or expensive. Washed and *thoroughly* dried glass jars are perfect, as are storage bags. Just make sure everything is airtight. Hang on to glass jars that have contained things like pasta sauce, pickles, and olives. Just wash and dry them and they're ready to house your dehydrated foods.

Some people like to make sure their dried foods are completely protected by using oxygen packs. These come in three sizes: 100 cc, 300 cc, and 500 cc, depending on what size jar you're using. A pack of 100 costs under $11, and many online sites sell them. Place a pack inside the jar or container and they absorb any residual oxygen that might be still lurking. When you open the jar you should hear a pop; that tells you that all the oxygen was sucked out by the pack. Another option, also sold at many sites, are Mylar bags, for added protection. The Mylar bags, which are made of the same materials as the balloons, are great for keeping air out of the food.

......................................................................................................................

**Label What You Save**
Don't forget to label everything with information about contents and the date the food was dried. If you're of a creative bent, you can even make the labels artistic—or not.

......................................................................................................................

One last rule: Choose a container that fits your quantity of food snugly. If you have one cup of raisins to store, opt for a one-cup container. Any extra air, even in an airtight container, has trace amounts of moisture that can ruin dehydrated foods. Fill your container so there's no space around the food.

If you want to go one step further you can use a vacuum packaging machine. This will allow you to store items in either bags or containers. The machine pulls out all the oxygen that can spoil food. Just like the dehydrating machines, vacuum packaging machines range in price from under $20 to around $150, depending on what type you pick.

## Where to Store Dehydrated Food

While dehydrated foods aren't particularly fussy about storage, a dark dry environment is what they like best. The pantry is a perfect storage area, as is a spare bedroom. The temperature should be fairly consistent since changing it too often can result in moisture building up inside the container. Unless you're going to use the dehydrated foods within a month, the kitchen isn't the best place for them. It's too moist and has temperature swings.

You can also store your dried foods in the freezer. There is less moisture there and the temperature is constant. Most people like to keep dried meats and fish in the freezer rather than in the pantry. Never store your dried foods in the fridge as there's too much ambient moisture there and you're constantly changing the temperature when you open and shut the door throughout the day.

Dried foods taste great and can be used in just about any recipe, so they may not sit around long. Many people like to rotate them every month or so. If you can resist the urge to eat them, they're usually good for a year. (Although some people have kept them for up to ten years. Amazingly, they're still good!)

There are just three storage rules to remember:

1. Dehydrate enough for your needs.
2. Ensure the food is completely cool before storing it.
3. Properly seal out all the air.

### Pasteurize for Protection

Mold on dried food usually means it wasn't dehydrated long enough. If you dry foods outside, pasteurize them before storing just in case insects got inside. To do this, place the foods in an oven at 175°F for fifteen minutes or in the freezer for a week.

## REHYDRATING DRIED FOOD

Many dried foods can be eaten as is, including dried fruits, leathers, and jerkies. However, others need to be reconstituted before eating.

There are several ways to put the water content back in dried food.

- Soak the food in cool water for two hours.
- Place the food in boiling water, cover, and simmer it for about fifteen minutes.
- Steam the food for five minutes.
- Use the food in a recipe in its dried form—for instance in your slow cooker.

If you're going the soaking route, use two cups of water for every one cup of dried vegetables and soak them for two hours. Most people use water to rehydrate foods, but you can also use stock, juice, and even milk. Note that unblanched foods take longer to reconstitute.

Let them stand until they look close to their original form before putting them into a recipe. When you substitute dried vegetables for fresh ones in any recipe, remember that one cup of dried vegetables equals about three cups fresh.

As you'll see in the third part of this book, one of the best ways to enjoy dried foods is to use them in recipes. Once foods have been rehydrated, of course, the cooking process is the same as fresh, frozen, and canned foods—although they will cook quicker if the food was blanched before you dried it.

**Too Much Water Is Bad**

One mistake many people make is to add too much water. Remember, *you can always add more water, but it's much harder to take it away once you've added it.* So add it a small bit at a time and be cautious.

Here are some other tips on rehydrating that will help you achieve perfect results.

- You shouldn't add salt because that can slow the rehydrating process.
- Since starch turns to sugar during drying and fruit sugars get more concentrated when they've been dried, don't add any more sugar.

- Vegetables are better if they are soaked to reabsorb their water before you add them to a recipe. They also take longer to rehydrate than fruits because they lose more water when they're dried.
- When soaking foods to rehydrate them, don't leave them out of the fridge longer than a couple of hours. Bacteria can start to grow.
- If you choose to add dried veggies to a recipe without rehydrating them, use one additional cup of water in your recipe for every cup of dried veggies you use. If you're making soup, use two cups of water for every one cup of dried veggies.
- Don't waste the soaking liquid because you can use it in other recipes too.
- You can reconstitute meat and poultry and use them in recipes. However, most people avoid using dried fish because it's salty and best eaten just as it is.

# PART II

# Dehydrating Vegetables, Fruits, Meats, Fish, Herbs, and Dairy

Let's start dehydrating. In this part, we'll show you how to dehydrate such goodies as shallots, ginger, pears, cranberries, and seafood. We'll also show you how to make your own mouthwatering jerkies.

# CHAPTER 4
# Vegetables

With many of us struggling to eat our recommended servings of vegetables, the dehydrator provides a welcome solution to that challenge. By having dehydrated vegetables on hand, you can quickly add a nutritional boost to soups, salads, and smoothies. In addition, you may find that you enjoy eating dried veggies as is—dried green beans and corn are wonderfully crisp and sweet. You'll be eating healthy as you snack.

# Beets

Dried beets are sweet, crunchy, and incredibly colorful. Drying beets retains the earthiness of the vegetable and extends its life. Use dried beets in their grated form or pulverize them into a powder and use as a coloring agent.

## Ingredients

½ pound fresh beet roots

........................................................................................................................................

**1.** Remove leafy greens from beets, if still attached, and reserve for another use. Using a very sharp knife, peel beets, discarding peels.

**2.** Grate beets on the largest hole of a box grater.

**3.** Spread beet pieces in a single even layer across one or more dehydrator shelves. Dry at 125°F until dried beet will snap in half when you bend it, about 5–6 hours.

**4.** Transfer beets to a clean work surface and cool to room temperature, about 2 hours. Transfer to an airtight container and store.

## Uses

- Add a handful of dried beets to your next smoothie that contains red fruits. The color of the beets will enhance the color of your drink, and the beets' sweetness will amplify the flavor of strawberry, cherry, or raspberry.
- Make beet powder by pulverizing dried beets in a spice grinder or small food processor. The beet powder is terrific added to prepared horseradish to make beet horseradish.
- Make a quick chilled beet soup. In a blender or food processor, blend dried beets with unflavored yogurt or sour cream. Thin with milk to desired consistency and add salt and pepper to taste. Serve with additional dried beets and dried dill as a garnish.
- Make beet chips: Instead of grating the beets, slice them into ⅛" slices. Dehydrate until crisp and eat in place of potato chips.

# Broccoli

*Despite its nutritional benefits, broccoli doesn't have too many fans. Many people have had barely steamed broccoli, or broccoli that is overcooked and the color of old khaki. Dried broccoli can be an appealing alternative. It offers the crunch and green color of raw broccoli but has a slightly tempered flavor, which can make it a secret healthy ingredient in many recipes.*

### Ingredients

1 large head broccoli

**1.** Wash broccoli and pat dry. Remove stems and discard. Cut broccoli into ¼" dice.

**2.** Spread broccoli pieces in a single even layer across one or more dehydrator shelves. Dry at 125°F until dried broccoli will snap in half when you bend it, about 6–8 hours.

**3.** Transfer broccoli to a clean work surface and cool to room temperature, about 2 hours. Transfer to an airtight container and store.

### Uses

- Add chopped dried broccoli to the ricotta cheese filling in your favorite lasagna recipe. The broccoli will soften as the lasagna cooks, and most of your diners will suspect it's the usual parsley.
- Make a green smoothie: Add 2 tablespoons dried broccoli to your favorite smoothie recipe to add fiber and vitamins. A terrific green smoothie recipe is 1 cup apple juice, ½ banana, 2 tablespoons dried broccoli, ½ teaspoon dried ginger, and ½ cup ice. Blend until completely smooth, about 3 minutes.
- Dried broccoli helps make a quick broccoli-cheese soup. Simmer ¼ cup dried broccoli per cup chicken stock until soft, about 30 minutes. Stir in ¼ cup grated aged Cheddar cheese until cheese is completely melted. To thicken the soup, stir 1 teaspoon cold water with 1 teaspoon cornstarch and add to soup.

# Cabbage

*It's easy to have a lot of cabbage on hand. After all, a single head of cabbage seems to make gallons of coleslaw. When you find yourself with leftover fresh cabbage, dehydrating is a terrific preservation technique. Dried cabbage can quickly go into soups or stir-fries.*

## Ingredients

1 medium head green or red cabbage

.................................................................................................................................

**1.** Wash cabbage and remove any outer leaves that are excessively loose or wilted. Cut cabbage into quarters. Cut out the core of each quarter and discard. Grate cabbage on the largest hole of a box grater.

**2.** Spread cabbage pieces in a single even layer across one or more dehydrator shelves. Dry at 125°F until dried cabbage will snap in half when you bend it, about 2–3 hours.

**3.** Transfer cabbage to a clean work surface and cool to room temperature, about 2 hours. Transfer to an airtight container and store.

## Uses

- Make egg rolls at home. Rehydrate cabbage and drain, squeezing out excess water. Mix with chopped cooked shrimp, chicken, or pork, crushed garlic, powdered ginger, and peanut butter that's been thinned with water. Roll in egg roll wrappers and fry in peanut oil.
- Make quick pierogi (Polish dumplings) from dried cabbage. Rehydrate cabbage and drain. Sauté in butter and add a sprinkling of salt and caraway seeds. Put a scant teaspoon onto a wonton wrapper, fold in half, and seal. Steam for 2–3 minutes and serve with sour cream.

# Carrots

*Carrots are part of mirepoix, a combination of carrot, onion, and celery that traditional French cuisine uses as a base for many stocks and soups. Having dried carrots on hand means that you can easily whip up soups or broths because the work of peeling and chopping carrots is already done.*

## Ingredients

½ pound carrots

.........................................................................................................................

**1.** Peel carrots, discarding peels. Grate carrots on the largest hole of a box grater.

**2.** Spread carrot pieces in a single even layer across one or more dehydrator shelves. Dry at 125°F until dried carrot will snap in half when you bend it, about 2–3 hours.

**3.** Transfer carrots to a clean work surface and cool to room temperature, about 2 hours. Transfer to an airtight container and store.

## Uses

- Make a quick stock by simmering equal parts of dried carrots, dried onions, and dried celery, covered by 1" water. To make a vegetable stock, simmer this combination with other dried vegetables, such as tomatoes, spinach, broccoli, and/or mushrooms, for 1 hour. For meat or chicken stock, simmer meat or chicken bones with dried carrots, onions, and celery for 6 hours. Strain and use in place of store-bought stock.
- Add dried carrot to your favorite green salad recipe to add a dash of color, sweetness, and nutrition. Dried carrot works nicely with both cream-style and vinegar-based salad dressings.
- Perk up coleslaw by adding a sprinkling of dried grated carrot to the fresh cabbage and dressing. The dressing will rehydrate the dried carrot.

# Corn

*Dehydrated corn is one of the most addictive foods on the planet. It's sweet, crunchy, and easy to eat—you'll find that you want to snack on it plain or by the handful. Dried corn is also a great addition to salads, salsas, and soups. It's a great way to bring the taste of summer to any day of the year.*

## Ingredients

4 ears corn

........................................................................................

**1.** Remove husks and silk from ears of corn. Wash corn and pat dry.

**2.** Using a sharp knife, remove kernels of corn from the cob in long, 1"–2" wide strips.

**3.** Spread corn kernels in a single even layer across one or more dehydrator shelves. Dry at 125°F until corn kernels crush easily between your fingertips, about 5–7 hours.

**4.** Transfer corn to a clean work surface and cool to room temperature, about 2 hours. Transfer to an airtight container and store.

## Uses

- Add texture and sweetness to corn bread or muffins. Prepare your favorite corn bread recipe, and stir dried corn right into the batter. Bake as usual and enjoy a crispy, sweet surprise.

- Make a quick corn salsa from dried corn. Mix 1 cup dried corn with 2 tablespoons fresh lime juice, 1 tablespoon corn oil, ¼ cup chopped onion, and ¼ cup chopped fresh cilantro. Season to taste with salt and pepper. Add fresh jalapeño peppers, or dried jalapeños, if desired.

- Grind dried corn into a powder and use in place of commercial corn meal.

........................................................................................

### More Corn!

Visit a farm stand and pick up some extra corn just for drying. You'll find it used in many of the recipes in Part III of this book—everything from chowder to bean and corn chips. In the dead of winter turn to frozen corn. Defrost a bag, drain, and place it onto the dehydrator, and in a couple of hours you have a good supply of dry corn.

........................................................................................

# Garlic

*Many stores sell peeled garlic cloves, which seem to go bad before you have a chance to use them all. Not to worry—dehydrating garlic is a terrific way to enjoy it. Not only are garlic slices useful, you can also make your own garlic powder for a fraction of the cost of the commercial product.*

### Ingredients
2 large heads of garlic or 20 cloves garlic

.................................................................................................................................................

**1.** Remove papery skins from garlic and discard. Cut garlic into ¼" slices.

**2.** Spread garlic slices in a single even layer across one or more dehydrator shelves. Dry at 125°F until dried garlic will snap in half when you bend it, about 3–4 hours.

**3.** Transfer garlic to a clean work surface and cool to room temperature, about 2 hours. Transfer to an airtight container and store.

### Uses

• Make garlic powder by pulverizing in a spice grinder or small food processor. Substitute one for one with commercial garlic powder. The garlic powder you make will be fresher than store-bought, and will be without preservatives or anti-caking agents.

• To make garlic mashed potatoes, add a few slices dried garlic to potatoes as you're boiling them. Proceed with your favorite mashed potato recipe.

• Stir into your favorite bottled ranch salad dressing to make garlic ranch.

• Powder and sprinkle onto chicken, fish, or pork. This way, you can cut the amount of salt you usually use for seasoning.

---

#### A Great Starter Vegetable

One way to make sure you have vegetables on hand to dehydrate is to grow them yourself. An easy one for the beginner is garlic. Plant it in the fall and enjoy it in spring and into summer too. It's perfect for eating fresh and ideal for drying. And don't forget the garlic scapes, the shoots that emerge above ground in spring. Use them as you would the actual garlic.

---

# Onions

*Dehydrated onion is a wonderful ingredient to have on hand. It rounds out the flavor of soups, stews, and broths, can be used to make a quick dip, and is delicious when sprinkled on vegetables. The trick is to slice the onions thinly and dehydrate them until they snap. This will preserve them best and will also make them easy to pulverize into homemade onion powder.*

### Ingredients
2 large yellow, white, or red onions

..................................................................................................................................

**1.** Remove papery skins from onions and discard. Cut onions into ¼" slices.

**2.** Spread onion slices in a single even layer across one or more dehydrator shelves. Dry at 125°F until dried onion will snap in half when you bend it, about 6–7 hours.

**3.** Transfer onions to a clean work surface and cool to room temperature, about 2 hours. Transfer to an airtight container and store.

### Uses

- Sprinkle dried onion slices on top of your favorite green bean casserole recipe to add the flavor and crunch of fried onions without extra calories and fat.

- Make a quick French onion soup by simmering ½ cup dried onions per 2 cups of your favorite beef broth for a half hour. Stir in 1 teaspoon brandy, if desired. Top with a slice of toasted French bread and a slice of Swiss cheese. Broil until cheese is melted, about 90 seconds.

- Make onion powder by pulverizing in a spice grinder or small food processor. Substitute one for one with commercial onion powder. You can make red onion powder, which tastes like regular onion powder but isn't sold in stores. Red onion adds a splash of color to any recipe.

# Scallions

*Green onions, or scallions, are fragile in their fresh state and don't last very long in the refrigerator. Plus, recipes often call for just a few scallions, leaving you with half a bunch or more that can spoil in your produce drawer. Dehydrating scallions is a way to extend the shelf life of these delicate vegetables. You can rehydrate them and use them as a substitute for fresh when you need just a small quantity of scallions.*

## Ingredients

1 bunch scallions

........................................................................................................................

**1.** Wash scallions and pat dry. Cut off root ends and any withered green tops, and discard. Cut scallions into ¼" slices.

**2.** Spread scallion slices in a single even layer across one or more dehydrator shelves. Dry at 125°F until dried scallion will snap in half when you bend it, about 2–3 hours.

**3.** Transfer scallions to a clean work surface and cool to room temperature, about 2 hours. Transfer to an airtight container and store.

## Uses

- Add crunch to any stir-fry by tossing a handful of dried scallions on top.
- Stir into cream cheese to create a quick sandwich spread.
- Powder and use as a slightly sweeter alternative to commercial onion powder.
- When baking bread, remove bread from the oven 10 minutes before it's done. Brush with vegetable oil and sprinkle on dried scallions.

# Shallots

*This is another ingredient used in small quantities; you may find yourself with leftover shallots and no immediate use for them. Luckily, these vegetables (which taste like a cross between onion and garlic) dry very well and are versatile in their dehydrated form.*

## Ingredients
5–6 large shallots

..................................................................................................................................

**1.** Remove papery skins from shallots and discard. Cut shallots into ¼" slices.
**2.** Spread shallot slices in a single even layer across one or more dehydrator shelves. Dry at 125°F until dried shallot will snap in half when you bend it, about 6–7 hours.
**3.** Transfer shallots to a clean work surface and cool to room temperature, about 2 hours. Transfer to an airtight container and store.

## Uses
- Make a quick beurre blanc (French white butter) sauce. Steep 1 tablespoon dried shallots in ½ cup white wine overnight. Bring to a boil and reduce to 1 tablespoon. Whisk in 8 pats ice-cold butter. Serve over vegetables, fish, or poultry.
- Shake with your favorite vinaigrette to add a true French flair.
- Add to your favorite egg salad recipe for a satisfying crunch.
- Use as a garnish with soups from Vietnam, such as pho or hot and sour soup. Vietnamese recipes rely on shallots more often than they use onions, so dried shallots offer a more authentic taste.

# Ginger

*Dehydrating ginger and making your own ginger powder is a great way to showcase the best in dehydrating. First, ginger dries beautifully and quickly. Second, homemade powdered ginger is more pungent than commercial ginger, meaning you can use less. Once you use dried ginger, you may never go back to buying bottled ginger powder.*

### Ingredients
3 (2"–3") pieces fresh gingerroot

**1.** Peel papery skins from ginger and discard. Cut ginger into ¼" slices.

**2.** Spread ginger slices in a single even layer across one or more dehydrator shelves. Dry at 125°F until dried ginger will snap in half when you bend it, about 4–6 hours.

**3.** Transfer ginger to a clean work surface and cool to room temperature, about 2 hours. Transfer to an airtight container and store.

### Uses

- Make ginger powder by pulverizing in a spice grinder or small food processor. Substitute two parts homemade ginger for every three parts called for of commercial ginger powder. (The exception is recipes in this book that call for homemade ginger powder.)

- Make sachets of mulling spices: Put 2 slices dried ginger, 1 slice dried citrus fruit, 3 cloves, 3 cardamom pods, 3 black peppercorns, and 1 star anise into cheesecloth and secure with twine. To mull wine or cider, bring 1 quart wine or cider to a boil. Add one sachet and simmer 30 minutes. Serve warm.

### Cure for Stomachaches
Ginger can ease nausea. To make ginger tea, pour boiling water over 2–3 slices dehydrated ginger. Steep 10 minutes, remove ginger, and drink.

# Green Beans

*If you like the crunch of fresh green beans, you're going to love dried green beans. Dehydrated green beans are the perfect healthy snack for someone on the go, replacing chips or pretzels. They also can be used in place of fresh or frozen green beans in recipes.*

## Ingredients
½ pound green beans

..................................................................................................................................

**1.** Wash beans and pat dry. Snap off ends and discard.

**2.** Spread whole beans in a single even layer across one or more dehydrator shelves. Dry at 125°F until dried bean will snap in half when you bend it, about 8–10 hours.

**3.** Transfer beans to a clean work surface and cool to room temperature, about 2 hours. Transfer to an airtight container and store.

## Uses

- Make three-bean salad: Rehydrate dried green beans overnight in vinegar. Drain, reserving vinegar. Add cooked dried chickpeas and cooked dried kidney beans to green beans. Make your favorite vinaigrette with the reserved vinegar, oil, salt, pepper, and sugar. Toss with beans and garnish with finely chopped red onion.

- Dehydrated green beans make a terrific savory trail mix. Mix equal parts dried green beans, toasted almonds, dried tomato halves, and dried corn. Divide into individual zippered bags and take on a hike for a vitamin-packed snack.

- Use dehydrated green beans instead of crackers or chips as a dipper for your favorite spinach or French onion dip.

# Kale Chips

*Natural grocery stores (and even some traditional stores) have shelves full of kale chips. These low-calorie, nutrient-dense chips are a great example of a healthy snack. With a dehydrator, you can make your own kale chips quickly and easily, saving money, and also giving yourself the ability to create the chip flavors you enjoy most.*

### Ingredients
1 large bunch kale
½ teaspoon olive oil
½ teaspoon salt
¼ teaspoon dried chili powder (optional)

1. Wash kale and pat dry. Remove and discard stems. Tear leaves into 2" squares.
2. Toss kale leaves with oil, salt, and optional chili powder. Toss well to ensure even coating.
3. Spread kale in a single even layer across one or more dehydrator shelves. Dry at 125°F until leaves crumble easily when rubbed between fingertips, about 2–3 hours.
4. Transfer kale to a clean work surface and cool to room temperature, about 2 hours. Transfer to an airtight container and store.

### Uses
- Make Mexican kale chips: Toss kale with ½ teaspoon canola oil, ½ teaspoon salt, ½ teaspoon cumin, ¼ teaspoon dried oregano, and ¼ teaspoon chili powder before dehydrating.
- Make Italian kale chips: Toss kale with ½ teaspoon extra-virgin olive oil, ½ teaspoon salt, 2 tablespoons finely grated Parmesan cheese, 1 teaspoon dried tomato powder, and ½ teaspoon dried basil before dehydrating.
- Make Asian kale chips: Toss kale with ½ teaspoon sesame oil, ½ teaspoon salt, ½ teaspoon dried garlic powder, ¼ teaspoon dried ginger powder, and 1 teaspoon toasted sesame seeds before dehydrating.

# Mushrooms

*Humans can distinguish five flavors: salty, sweet, sour, bitter, and umami, which roughly translates to "savory" or "meaty." Mushrooms are an excellent source of umami flavor, making them essential for creating vegetarian dishes that even meat lovers will crave.*

## Ingredients

1 pound mushrooms, such as white mushrooms, Portobello, shiitake, or oyster

........................................................................................................

**1.** Wipe the cap of each mushroom with a clean, damp cloth. Remove stems and reserve for another usage.

**2.** Spread mushroom caps in a single even layer across one or more dehydrator shelves. Dry at 135°F until dried mushroom will snap in half when you bend it, about 3–4 hours.

**3.** Transfer mushrooms to a clean work surface and cool to room temperature, about 2 hours. Transfer to an airtight container and store.

## Uses

- Make a quick mushroom-barley soup: Simmer equal parts of barley and dried mushrooms covered by an inch of flavorful stock, such as beef, vegetable, or chicken. Cook until barley is done, about 45 minutes to an hour. Add salt and pepper to taste.

- Rehydrate mushrooms, drain, and sauté until golden in olive oil or butter. Add fresh garlic and fresh herbs such as thyme or rosemary and sauté an additional minute. Toss over cooked pasta and serve with grated Parmesan.

- Powdered dried mushrooms are a ready (and vegetarian) substitute for Worcestershire sauce, which contains fish. Replace one for one in recipes.

- Rehydrate mushrooms and use to top your next frozen pizza.

# Bell Peppers

*At the end of the summer, peppers ripen faster than you can use them. To preserve this healthy summer vegetable, dry roughly half of your bumper crop. Dried peppers take a fraction of the space of canned or frozen peppers. As well, you can create an on-the-fly chili from dried peppers whenever the mood strikes.*

### Ingredients
2–3 large bell peppers (any color)

**1.** Wash peppers and pat dry. Remove stems and seeds and discard. Cut peppers into ½" dice.

**2.** Spread pepper pieces in a single even layer across one or more dehydrator shelves. Dry at 125°F until dried pepper will snap in half when you bend it, about 4–6 hours.

**3.** Transfer peppers to a clean work surface and cool to room temperature, about 2 hours. Transfer to an airtight container and store.

### Uses

- Make a quick, brightly colored dip. Mix equal parts mayonnaise and either sour cream or plain Greek yogurt. Add a dash of Worcestershire sauce and a pinch of salt. Stir in dried bell peppers of all colors. Refrigerate 30 minutes and serve with cut veggies and crackers.

- Powder dried red bell peppers in your spice grinder or food processor and use as a substitute for paprika.

- Add flavor and nutrients to canned chili by heating up the chili, stirring in some dried peppers, and letting the peppers soften 10 minutes.

# Small Chili Peppers

*Ethnic grocery stores sell chili peppers in large quantities, which often leaves you scrambling to use them before they go bad. You can take a cue from Native Americans and Southwesterners and dry your peppers. However, instead of hanging chili peppers to dry, use your dehydrator.*

### Ingredients

20–25 small chili peppers (such as Thai chilies, cayenne, or Serrano)

......................................................................................................................

**1.** Wash peppers and pat dry.
**2.** Spread whole peppers in a single even layer across one or more dehydrator shelves. Dry at 125°F until dried pepper will snap in half when you bend it, about 8–10 hours.
**3.** Transfer peppers to a clean work surface and cool to room temperature, about 2 hours. Transfer to an airtight container and store.

### Uses

- Make hot chili powder by pulverizing in a spice grinder or small food processor. Substitute one for one with commercial chili powder. Keep each type of pepper separate and labeled so that you can experiment with which pepper variety works best in your favorite recipes.
- Add a small pinch of dried chilies to your favorite chocolate dessert. The spice will accentuate the richness of your chocolate and leave your guests wondering what your mystery ingredient is. Be sure to use it very sparingly, as too much chili pepper can overwhelm a dessert, and make it less than a treat.
- Infuse vodka for spicy Bloody Marys. Place 4–6 small chili peppers into a 750 ml bottle of unflavored vodka. Steep at room temperature for 2–3 weeks. Strain out peppers and enjoy in your favorite vodka-based drink recipe.

# Jalapeño Peppers
## (or Other Medium to Large Hot Chili Peppers)

*When bell peppers are in season, so are jalapeño and banana peppers. Take advantage of lower prices by buying these hot peppers in bulk and dehydrating them. Not only do they rehydrate nicely, but you can use them to make homemade chili powder that is simply dried chili pepper, unlike commercial chili powder, which often contains other herbs, garlic, sugar, or salt.*

### Ingredients
8–10 medium to large hot chili peppers (such as jalapeño, Anaheim, banana pepper, cherry pepper, or habanero)

......................................................................................................................

**1.** Wash peppers and pat dry. Remove stems and seeds and discard. Cut peppers into ¼" slices.

**2.** Spread pepper slices in a single even layer across one or more dehydrator shelves. Dry at 125°F until dried pepper will snap in half when you bend it, about 6–7 hours.

**3.** Transfer peppers to a clean work surface and cool to room temperature, about 2 hours. Transfer to an airtight container and store.

### Uses
- Spice up any chili recipe by swapping out dried hot chili pepper for half of the traditional bell peppers.
- Crumble over an Italian beef sandwich for spice and crunch.
- Add a few pieces of dried jalapeño to mild salsa to make it medium or hot.
- Make a hot and spicy dip for corn chips. Heat canned Cheddar cheese dip and add dried hot chili peppers. Let stand 10 minutes to soften the peppers and impart heat. Remove peppers if you'd like a milder dip, or leave peppers in for some serious heat.

# Peas

*To bring a hint of sweetness to savory recipes, just add peas. For this reason, many freezers have bags of trusty English peas that are used a handful at a time. Rather than use valuable freezer space, dry your next batch of English peas.*

## Ingredients
1 pound English peas

.........................................................................................................................

**1.** Remove peas from shells and discard shells. Place peas in a wire mesh strainer and rinse under cold running water.

**2.** Spread peas in a single even layer across one or more dehydrator shelves. Dry at 125°F until each pea is very hard, about 8–10 hours.

**3.** Transfer peas to a clean work surface and cool to room temperature, about 2 hours. Transfer to an airtight container and store.

## Uses
- Peas are integral to a rich pasta sauce. Simmer ¼ cup peas in 1 cup heavy cream until softened, about 30 minutes. Sauté ½ cup chopped ham in 1 teaspoon butter and add to sauce. Cook until cream is the consistency of honey. Season to taste with salt and pepper and serve over hot spaghetti, egg noodles, or linguine. Top with Parmesan.
- Cook peas until very soft and use in place of chickpeas in your favorite hummus recipe.
- Use dried English peas in place of dried split peas in your favorite split pea soup recipe.
- Make a quick and easy baby food: Pulverize dried peas in a spice grinder. Add 1 tablespoon dried pea powder to 1½ tablespoons warm water. Stir and serve.

# Potatoes

*Dried potatoes are perfect to keep on hand. They can be used to make quick soups, or as gluten-free thickening agents. They also add body to stews.*

## Ingredients
1 tablespoon fresh lemon juice
1 pound baking potatoes (such as russet or Yukon gold)

......................................................................................................................................

**1.** Fill a large bowl ¾ full with clean water and add lemon juice.
**2.** Peel potatoes, discarding peels. Place each peeled potato into the bowl of lemon water. Grate potatoes on the largest hole of a box grater, returning the grated potatoes to the bowl of lemon juice.
**3.** Drain potatoes through a wire mesh strainer and pat dry with paper towels.
**4.** Spread potato pieces in a single even layer across one or more dehydrator shelves. Dry at 125°F until dried potato will snap in half when you bend it, about 4–6 hours.
**5.** Transfer potatoes to a clean work surface and cool to room temperature, about 2 hours. Transfer to an airtight container and store.

## Uses
- For a gluten-free way to thicken sauces, soups, and stews, powder potatoes in a food processor and add 1 teaspoon potato powder per cup of liquid. Bring to a simmer, and cook until the potato starch releases and gels, about 20 minutes.
- Make crispy coatings for fried items by substituting dried potatoes for breadcrumbs.
- Use dried potatoes instead of fresh potatoes in your favorite stew recipe. For each cup of fresh potatoes, add ½ cup dried potatoes. Cook until potatoes are softened, about 20 minutes.

# Sweet Potatoes

*Sweet potatoes show up on many "healthiest foods" lists due to their high fiber content, high level of B vitamins and carotene, and anti-inflammatory properties. Having dried sweet potatoes on hand gives you the ability to put together a healthy side dish in minutes or even have a healthy snack.*

### Ingredients

1 pound sweet potatoes

**1.** Peel sweet potatoes, discarding peels. Cut potatoes into ⅛" slices. Spread potato slices in a single even layer across one or more dehydrator shelves. Dry at 125°F until dried potato will snap in half when you bend it, about 10–12 hours.

**2.** Transfer potatoes to a clean work surface and cool to room temperature, about 2 hours. Transfer to an airtight container and store.

### Uses

- Use this recipe to make sweet potato chips. Toss cut potatoes in 1 tablespoon vegetable oil, 1 teaspoon salt, and ½ teaspoon dried chili peppers (optional). Dehydrate as usual.
- Make sweet potato latkes by altering your favorite latke recipe. Rehydrate dried sweet potatoes in warm water for 20 minutes. Then drain and chop into a fine julienne. Follow latke recipe, using the prepared sweet potatoes in place of grated white potatoes.
- Make a quick and easy weeknight dinner. Simmer cut pieces of raw boneless skinless chicken breasts in chicken stock with a handful of dried sweet potatoes. Season to taste and enjoy with a fresh green salad.

# Spinach

*Delicate spinach leaves last only a few days when fresh. However, dehydrated spinach leaves can last months when stored properly. Keep dried spinach on hand to make healthy appetizers, dips, and side dishes.*

## Ingredients
1 pound spinach

**1.** Remove stems from spinach and discard stems. Wash spinach and spin dry in a salad spinner.
**2.** Spread in a single even layer across one or more dehydrator shelves. Dry at 125°F until spinach leaves crumble easily when rubbed between fingertips, about 90 minutes–3 hours.
**3.** Transfer spinach to a clean work surface and cool to room temperature, about 2 hours. Transfer to an airtight container and store.

## Uses
- Make a quick spinach dip: Add ¼ cup dried spinach to ½ cup light mayonnaise and ½ cup nonfat Greek yogurt. Add fresh lemon juice, salt, and pepper to taste. Serve with whole-grain crackers for a quick and healthy snack.
- Add dried spinach to your favorite smoothie recipe.

### A Healthy Smoothie
To make a spinach smoothie blend 1 tablespoon dried spinach with 1 cup orange juice, 1 whole banana, and a handful of fresh or frozen blueberries. The vitamin C in the orange juice helps your body make the most of the iron in the spinach. Plus the blueberries camouflage spinach's bright green hue.

- Powder dried spinach in a spice grinder or mini food processor. Use the powder to color pâtés or soft cheese. You can make a simple holiday torta with a block of cream cheese. Mix ⅓ of an 8-ounce block of cream cheese with 3 tablespoons dried powdered spinach. Mix the second ⅓ with dried tomato powder, and leave the last ⅓ of the cream cheese unflavored. Mold cheeses together—placing the green cream cheese at one end, the white cream cheese in the middle, and the red cream cheese at the other end. Serve with bagel chips.

# Tomatoes

*Tomatoes are versatile when dried. For a chewier consistency, dry them for a shorter amount of time, and then use them as the base for canapés or as a quick addition to an antipasto tray. Dry them for longer and you can make them into tomato powder, which you can rehydrate into tomato paste.*

### Ingredients

1 pint cherry, grape, or Roma tomatoes

.............................................................................................................................

**1.** Wash tomatoes and pat dry. Slice in half lengthwise.

**2.** Spread tomatoes in a single even layer, cut side down, across one or more dehydrator shelves. Dry at 125°F until dried tomato is dry to the touch, about 10–12 hours.

**3.** Transfer tomatoes to a clean work surface and cool to room temperature, about 2 hours. Transfer to an airtight container and store.

### Uses

- Dry completely and pulverize into powder. Use tomato powder as a substitute for paprika to give the same color and a slightly sweeter taste.
- Stir equal parts tomato powder and water to create tomato paste. Use as a substitute for canned tomato paste.
- Quickly boost flavor in tomato sauces by adding either chopped dried tomatoes or tomato powder 5 minutes before the end of cooking. Dried tomatoes add umami, which translates from Japanese as "savory flavor" and can often make vegetarian dishes taste heartier.

# CHAPTER 5
# Fruits

Some of nature's best-tasting foods, fruits are also the most fleeting when it comes to perfect ripeness. You can capture the summer-sweetness of perfectly ripe berries or stone fruit, the tropical goodness of mango and papaya, or the crisp fall taste of apples and pears by dehydrating fruits when they are at the peak of flavor. Use your dried fruit to create desserts or to add a sweet note to otherwise savory dishes.

# Apples

*A backpacker's staple, dehydrated apples are versatile and delicious. You can dry them to a crisp and use as apple chips, or dehydrate them to a lesser degree and use in both sweet and savory recipes.*

## Ingredients

1 tablespoon fresh lemon juice

1 pound apples

.......................................................................................................................

**1.** Fill a large bowl ¾ full with clean water and add lemon juice.

**2.** Place each peeled apple into the bowl of lemon water.

**3.** Cut each apple in half lengthwise. Using a melon baller, remove seed pack from apple. Return cut apples to water with lemon juice.

**4.** Slice each apple half into ⅛"-thin slices. Return apple slices to water with lemon juice.

**5.** Drain apples through a wire mesh strainer and pat dry with paper towels.

**6.** Spread apple pieces in a single even layer across one or more dehydrator shelves. Dry at 135°F until dried apple will snap in half when you bend it, about 4–6 hours.

**7.** Transfer apples to a clean work surface and cool to room temperature, about 2 hours. Transfer to an airtight container and store.

## Uses

- Use dehydrated apples instead of raisins in your favorite granola, cookie, and quick bread recipes. A one-to-one substitution is perfect, and will add a slight tang to the recipe.
- Make a Turkish treat—apple tea: Steep 2 tablespoons dried apples in 6 ounces of boiling water for 20 minutes. Drain and sweeten, if desired, with honey.
- Toss over your favorite green salad, along with goat cheese and toasted pecans. Serve with balsamic vinaigrette dressing.

.......................................................................................................................

### Banish Brown Apples

Sometimes not even lemon juice can prevent apples from browning as they dry. While it doesn't affect their taste, the look isn't attractive. One nice addition, especially in fall when apples are abundant, is apple cider. No more brown apples, and it imparts a wonderful flavor.

.......................................................................................................................

# Apricots

*The main difference between dried apricots you buy in a store and ones you make at home are the preserving agents used in store-bought apricots. In order to help apricots retain their light orange color, commercial processors use sulphur. A squeeze of fresh lemon juice will help to retain the color when you dry apricots at home, though, and won't produce any off flavors.*

## Ingredients
1 tablespoon fresh lemon juice
1 pound apricots

...........................................................................................................................

**1.** Fill a large bowl ¾ full with clean water and add lemon juice.
**2.** Wash and dry apricots. Split in half lengthwise. Remove and discard pits. Place apricot halves into bowl of lemon juice and water. Let soak 5 minutes.
**3.** Drain apricots and spread in a single even layer, cut side down, across one or more dehydrator shelves. Dry at 135°F until reduced in size and dry but still chewy, about 14–16 hours.
**4.** Transfer apricots to a clean work surface and cool to room temperature, about 2 hours. Transfer to an airtight container and store.

## Uses
- Moroccan food relies on dried fruit—particularly apricots—to produce a sweet and savory effect in main dishes. To add Moroccan flavor to your meals, make a chicken stew or a chicken pot pie with dried apricots.
- A dried apricot is the perfect gluten-free substitute for crackers with a cheese tray. Half an apricot tastes lovely with brie, ricotta, or fresh goat cheese.
- Spear dried apricots along with pearl onions, green peppers, and chicken cubes for a new twist on grilled chicken skewers.

# Bananas

*Store-bought banana chips seem like a healthy indulgence. They're crunchy and full of fiber and vitamins, but many contain preservatives and extra sugar. To have a truly healthy banana chip, make yours at home, where the only two ingredients are bananas and orange juice, which serves to keep the bananas from browning.*

## Ingredients
4–5 bananas
½ cup orange juice

**1.** Peel bananas and cut into ¼" slices. Dip each slice into orange juice, shaking off excess.
**2.** Spread banana slices in a single even layer across one or more dehydrator shelves. Dry at 135°F until dried banana will snap in half when you bend it, about 16–18 hours.
**3.** Transfer bananas to a clean work surface and cool to room temperature, about 2 hours. Transfer to an airtight container and store.

## Uses
- Make a portable banana split dessert. Combine banana chips, dried cherries, dried pineapple, toasted pecans, and a few dark and/or white chocolate chips.
- Crush banana chips in a food processor or spice mill and use as a topping for desserts in place of chopped nuts.
- Cut bananas lengthwise and dehydrate as directed to make fiber-packed chewy treats for your dog. Cutting lengthwise will encourage your dog to chew on the dried banana like a dog bone.

# Blackberries

*Unless fresh blackberries are at their peak of ripeness, you run the risk of finding sour berries. Dehydrating solves this problem, as the evaporation process reduces the water content and intensifies the sweetness. Blackberry seeds, which can be problematic in fresh blackberries, also become an asset in the dried fruit, as they shrink slightly and get crisp along with the rest of the berry.*

### Ingredients

1 pint blackberries

........................................................................................................................

**1.** Wash berries and pat dry.

**2.** Spread berries in a single even layer across one or more dehydrator shelves. Dry at 125°F until berries crush easily between your fingertips, about 12–14 hours.

**3.** Transfer blackberries to a clean work surface and cool to room temperature, about 2 hours. Transfer to an airtight container and store.

### Uses

- A handful of dried blackberries adds sweetness, vitamins, and fiber to most breakfast cereals.
- Substitute blackberries for raisins in your favorite granola recipe. Look for recipes that have vanilla, almonds, and/or cinnamon as ingredients, as these flavors work well with blackberries.
- Make a quick pancake topping. Heat your favorite maple syrup to a simmer. Add a handful of dried blackberries and steep 10 minutes. They are especially delicious over buckwheat pancakes.

# Blueberries

*When blueberries come into season, they really come in abundance. Many cooks find that they run out of space to freeze berries, and grow tired of blueberry pies, smoothies, and jams. Dehydrating is another preservation option, and allows you the flexibility to use blueberries in a concentrated form in recipes.*

### Ingredients

1 pint blueberries

..................................................................................................................

**1.** Wash blueberries and pat dry.

**2.** Spread berries in a single even layer across one or more dehydrator shelves. Dry at 125°F until blueberries reduce in size by ¾ and are dry but still chewy, about 7–8 hours.

**3.** Transfer blueberries to a clean work surface and cool to room temperature, about 2 hours. Transfer to an airtight container and store.

### Uses

- Make blueberry vodka to add a hint of berry to plain vodka and soda. Pour 2 cups of vodka into a glass container and add ½ cup dried blueberries. Steep at room temperature for 2-3 weeks, then strain, discarding the blueberries. Use as a substitute for unflavored vodka in drinks such as Cosmopolitans and Vodka Collins.

- Add dried blueberries to pancake or waffle batter. You get the same great taste as you would with fresh blueberries, without turning the entire pancake blue. Or, if you're making a baked French toast casserole, add a handful of dried blueberries to the custard mix before pouring over the bread.

- Make a blueberry butter: Pulverize blueberries in your food processor or spice grinder. Add to softened butter and mix well. Roll into plastic wrap and place in refrigerator to harden. When ready to use, spread onto breakfast breads, or place slices of blueberry butter under the skin of a chicken as you roast it.

# Cantaloupe

*If you like fruit candy, dehydrated cantaloupe is for you. Sweet and lightly spicy, this dried fruit satisfies any sweet tooth in a healthy fashion. And it's not just limited to snacking. You can make hearty lunches and sweet treats with dried cantaloupe.*

### Ingredients
1 large cantaloupe

......................................................................................................................................

**1.** Wash cantaloupe. Cut in half crosswise. Remove seeds and discard. Peel cantaloupe, discarding peels.

**2.** Cut into ⅛" slices. Spread cantaloupe pieces in a single even layer across one or more dehydrator shelves. Dry at 135°F until dried cantaloupe will snap in half when you bend it, about 5–6 hours.

**3.** Transfer cantaloupe to a clean work surface and cool to room temperature, about 2 hours. Transfer to an airtight container and store.

### Uses
- Add dried cantaloupe to smoked turkey sandwiches. Layer whole-grain bread with mayonnaise, a layer of lettuce, and piles of smoked turkey. Top with 2–3 slices of cantaloupe for a sweet and crunchy delight. Skip the tomatoes and onions, as these two will overpower the cantaloupe. Also works well in the same sandwich with roasted turkey or honey ham.
- Soak cantaloupe in sweet white wine, such as Riesling or Moscato, until softened, about 20 minutes. Drain and use as a topping for rich vanilla ice cream. Terrific with coconut, caramel, or strawberry ice cream.
- Rehydrate dried cantaloupe and wrap around mozzarella cheese sticks or string cheese for a quick sweet and savory appetizer. If you like, also wrap with a slice of prosciutto.

# Cherries

*Both sweet and tart cherries make excellent dried fruit. While the sweet ones are similar to raisins, tart cherries have more in common with dried cranberries. Sweet cherries, like raisins, may be eaten plain and work well in desserts. Tart cherries are better in savory recipes, or taste delicious after rehydrating in a sweet liquid.*

## Ingredients

1 pound sweet or tart cherries

........................................................................................................................

**1.** Wash and dry cherries. Pit and split in half lengthwise. Discard pits.

**2.** Spread cherries in a single even layer, cut side down, across one or more dehydrator shelves. Dry at 135°F until reduced in size and dry but still chewy, about 10–12 hours.

**3.** Transfer cherries to a clean work surface and cool to room temperature, about 2 hours. Transfer to an airtight container and store.

## Uses

• Make your favorite rice pudding with dried cherries. Add cherries with the liquid, allowing the warm liquid to rehydrate the cherries as the rice cooks. Because the cherries will absorb a bit of liquid, you may need to add some milk in order to achieve the right consistency. Serve with a dusting of cinnamon, which heightens the flavor of the cherries.

• Chop dried cherries—either sweet or tart—and use as a garnish for grilled asparagus.

• Infuse bourbon with dried cherries. Place 2 cups bourbon in a glass container and add ½ cup dried cherries. Allow to steep 2-3 weeks, and then drain bourbon, discarding cherries. Use in an Old Fashioned, a Manhattan, or in a highball with ginger ale.

# Coconuts

*Mountains of fluffy dried coconut are on every cook's wish list—it goes so well into Southeast Asian curries, tropical desserts, and an iconic pie. When you dehydrate your own coconut, you have the ability to control the amount of sugar in the end result and can therefore have better control over your cooking and baking.*

### Ingredients
1 ripe coconut

**1.** Split coconut in half using a chef's knife or cleaver. Drain liquid and reserve for another use. Remove white coconut flesh from the inside of coconut, using a metal spoon.

**2.** Coarsely chop coconut flesh and spread in a single even layer across one or more dehydrator shelves. Dry at 135°F until dried coconut will snap in half when you bend it, about 10–12 hours.

**3.** Transfer coconut to a clean work surface and cool to room temperature, about 2 hours. Transfer to an airtight container and store.

### Uses
- Home-dehydrated coconut makes the best coating for coconut shrimp and coconut chicken because it doesn't contain added sugar, which makes it burn easily. Skewer cubes of raw chicken or raw peeled and deveined shrimp. Dust in flour seasoned with salt and pepper. Dip in beaten egg. Coat with dried coconut. Shallow-fry in vegetable oil until golden brown. For chicken, transfer skewers to a baking sheet and bake at 400°F for 4-5 minutes. Serve with curried mayonnaise.
- Toast coconut to use as a garnish on South Indian curries or Vietnamese curries that have coconut milk in the sauce. A dusting of toasted coconut really accentuates the creamy coconut flavor.
- Use coconut to rim a cocktail glass for cocktails such as Piña Coladas or Mai Tais.

# Cranberries

*Commercially prepared dried cranberries, also known as "craisins," are wildly popular and come in a variety of flavors, such as lemon and orange. However, they also contain a high amount of sugar and preserving ingredients. To take control of the amount of sugar in your dried cranberries, make them yourself.*

## Ingredients
1 cup sugar
½ cup water
1 (12-ounce) package fresh cranberries

**1.** Combine sugar and water. Bring to a boil and cook, without stirring, until sugar is just dissolved, about 5 minutes. Remove from heat and allow to cool completely, about 30 minutes.

**2.** Wash berries and pat dry. Cut each berry in half. Toss berries in sugar syrup.

**3.** Spread berries in a single even layer across one or more dehydrator shelves. Dry at 125°F until berries are ¾ their original size and are dry but still chewy, about 6–8 hours.

**4.** Transfer cranberries to a clean work surface and cool to room temperature, about 2 hours. Transfer to an airtight container and store.

## Uses

- Stir into smooth cranberry sauce to add an interesting texture, as well as a slightly different flavor. You can add dried cranberries to your own homemade sauce after it sets or add to the canned variety.

- Experiment with different flavorings when you dry your cranberries. When you make the sugar water, steep pieces of dried citrus fruit, or herbs such as sage or thyme. Let sit 20 minutes, strain, and use the flavored sugar water to coat the cranberries.

### Using That Leftover Sauce

If you have leftover cranberry sauce after Thanksgiving or other holiday meals, don't throw it away; instead, use it as an accompaniment to a cheese platter. It pairs perfectly with lots of cheeses and adds a splash of color to the buffet table.

# Figs

*Figs, like plums, undergo amazing changes as a result of dehydrating. With the drying process, figs go from sweet-sour juicy fruit with just a hint of grassy flavor to a richly textured fruit with hints of cinnamon and chocolate. Dried figs make a lovely mid-afternoon break when enjoyed with a cup of tea.*

### Ingredients

1 tablespoon fresh lemon juice
1 pound fresh figs

**1.** Fill a large bowl ¾ full with clean water and add lemon juice.

**2.** Wash and dry figs. Split in half lengthwise. Place fig halves into bowl of lemon juice and water. Let soak 5 minutes.

**3.** Drain figs and spread in a single even layer, cut side down, across one or more dehydrator shelves. Dry at 135°F until reduced in size and dry but still chewy, about 14–16 hours.

**4.** Transfer figs to a clean work surface and cool to room temperature, about 2 hours. Transfer to an airtight container and store.

### Uses

- Figs are great when rehydrated in port, brandy, or even bourbon. The slight flavor of alcohol brings out the baking spices in the flavor of dried figs. Once rehydrated, use the figs as a compote to garnish pound cake, rice pudding, or a lovely white cake. Use the residual liquor for cocktails.

- Make a riff on fresh figs with bleu cheese. Lay out a bed of your favorite salad greens, top with quartered dried figs, crumbled bleu cheese (or dehydrated bleu cheese), walnuts, and your favorite balsamic dressing.

# Grapefruit

*Plump, juicy grapefruit transforms into crisp, slightly translucent slices that look like stained glass windows when dehydrated. You can eat slices plain as a low-calorie treat, or use in luscious dessert recipes that require a slightly tart taste.*

## Ingredients
2 large grapefruits

........................................................................................................

**1.** Wash grapefruits and pat dry. Cut into ¼" slices.

**2.** Spread grapefruit slices in a single even layer across one or more dehydrator shelves. Dry at 135°F until dried grapefruit will snap in half when you bend it, about 12–14 hours.

**3.** Transfer grapefruits to a clean work surface and cool to room temperature, about 2 hours. Transfer to an airtight container and store.

## Uses

• Make a quick herbal tea. Break 1 slice dried grapefruit into pieces and place in a tea cup with a teaspoon of dried mint. Top with boiling water and steep 10 minutes. Strain and enjoy. Or make an entire pitcher of sun tea: Place 5-6 slices dried grapefruit into a pitcher with ¼ cup dried mint and fill with cold water. Cover tightly and place in a sunny spot all day. Strain out solids and refrigerate until chilled, about 2 hours.

• Break pieces of dried grapefruit and stir into apricot jam to make a sweet–tart treat. Use jam as a toast topper, in thumbprint cookies, or as a glaze for chicken breasts.

• Dried grapefruit makes an excellent body scrub. Roughly chop 3-4 slices dried grapefruit, mix with 1 cup Epsom salts, 1 tablespoon dried rosemary, and ½ cup neutral vegetable oil, such as sunflower seed oil. Store in a shatterproof container, such as a plastic jar. Use to scrub rough elbows and kneecaps.

# Guava

*Tropical guava is associated with vacations to exotic locales, but you can readily find guava in warmer parts of the United States, such as Florida, California, and Texas. If you live in a cooler climate, it's still relatively easy to buy fresh guava at an ethnic grocery store. When buying fresh guava, be sure to pick up a few extra. They dry easily and are great to stash in your cupboard for days you're pining for a warm-weather vacation.*

## Ingredients
1 tablespoon fresh lime juice
5–6 ripe guava

**1.** Fill a large bowl ¾ full with clean water and add lime juice.

**2.** Wash and dry guava. Peel guava, if desired. Slice guava into ¼"-thick slices. Place guava into bowl of lime juice and water. Let soak 5 minutes.

**3.** Drain guava slices and spread in a single even layer across one or more dehydrator shelves. Dry at 135°F until reduced in size and dry but still chewy, about 10–12 hours.

**4.** Transfer guava to a clean work surface and cool to room temperature, about 2 hours. Transfer to an airtight container and store.

## Uses
- The sweetness of dried guava makes it the perfect foil for tangy desserts. You can chop dried guava finely and use it to decorate the side of a New York–style cheesecake. Or you can rehydrate guava and use to decorate the top of a cheesecake or key lime pie.
- Guava pairs nicely with fish or chicken. Add cubed dried guava to your favorite stuffing recipe (it's especially good with rice stuffings) or lay slices of dried guava on top of fish as you bake it.

# Kiwis

*The color and flavor of a fresh kiwi both intensify when you dry it, resulting in a super-sweet fruit that is an ethereal shade of green. Due to their color, dried kiwis are great for decorating desserts, but they're also great in a variety of savory dishes.*

### Ingredients
5–6 ripe kiwi fruit

.........................................................................................................................

**1.** Peel kiwis and discard peel. Slice kiwi into ¼"-thick slices.

**2.** Spread kiwi slices in a single even layer across one or more dehydrator shelves. Dry at 135°F until reduced in size and dry but still chewy, about 10–12 hours.

**3.** Transfer kiwi to a clean work surface and cool to room temperature, about 2 hours. Transfer to an airtight container and store.

### Uses

- Make mini sorbet sandwiches with dried kiwi. Take your favorite fruit-flavored sorbet—tropical flavors such as pineapple, coconut, or mango work well with kiwi—and allow it to soften at room temperature for 5 minutes. Scoop 1 tablespoon sorbet on top of a slice of kiwi and top with a second slice of dried kiwi. Press together slightly and wrap in plastic. Return to freezer and freeze until firm, about 1 hour.

- Dried kiwi complements the flavor of richer meats, such as lamb or venison. Chop dried kiwi coarsely and rehydrate in warm water. Drain and serve atop slices of roast lamb.

- Use dried kiwis instead of fresh kiwis to decorate a fruit tart. You can rehydrate the fruit first to create a softer texture, or leave dehydrated for a chewier consistency.

# Kumquats

*Tiny, one-bite kumquats are bursting with a multitude of flavors—bitter rind and sweet-tart pulp. Dried, they hold the same appeal and offer a smaller alternative to dried orange slices. You can use as a substitute for any dried citrus or for orange zest in recipes.*

## Ingredients
1 pint kumquats

1. Wash kumquats and pat dry. Cut into ¼" slices.
2. Spread kumquats in a single even layer across one or more dehydrator shelves. Dry at 135°F until dried kumquat will snap in half when you bend it, about 5–6 hours.
3. Transfer kumquats to a clean work surface and cool to room temperature, about 2 hours. Transfer to an airtight container and store.

## Uses
- Because they are naturally small in diameter, dried kumquat slices are terrific to use whole. Float them dramatically across a punch bowl in either summer or winter. Add them to potpourri, or decorate homemade candles with them.
- Stir dried kumquat slices into store-bought or homemade lemon sorbet to add color, crunch, and depth of flavor. Remove sorbet from refrigerator and let stand in your sink for 5 minutes. Stir in slices of dried kumquat and serve.
- Candy slices of dried kumquat. Make a simple syrup by boiling equal parts of water and granulated sugar. Add slices of kumquat and simmer until reduced all the way. Dry kumquats on a wire rack and use candied kumquats to decorate a yellow cake or cheesecake.

# Lemons

*Many cooks prize lemon zest as much as they do lemon juice. With dehydrated lemon, you get the best of both—the intense lemon flavor of the zest, and the acidity of the juice. It's great to have dehydrated lemon on hand to save you the trouble of zesting and/or juicing lemons when you're short on time.*

## Ingredients
5–6 lemons

........................................................................................................................................

**1.** Wash lemons and pat dry. Cut into ¼" slices.
**2.** Spread lemons in a single even layer across one or more dehydrator shelves. Dry at 135°F until dried lemon will snap in half when you bend it, about 6–7 hours.
**3.** Transfer lemons to a clean work surface and cool to room temperature, about 2 hours. Transfer to an airtight container and store.

## Uses

- Make homemade lemon pepper. Pulverize dried lemon slices in a spice grinder or small food processor. Add in equal parts to ground black pepper or ground white pepper. Use as a one-to-one substitute for commercial lemon pepper.
- Add gourmet flair to your next fish fry. Crush 1–2 dried lemon slices into your usual breadcrumbs and use in your favorite fish-breading recipe.
- Turn your side-dish blues into sunny side dishes. Rehydrate lemon slices, drain, and sauté in olive oil or butter until golden. Add dried or fresh garlic and cook 30 seconds. Use as a topping for green vegetables, such as broccoli, cabbage, or asparagus.
- Easy Thanksgiving side dish to make while your turkey rests: Preheat oven to 425°F. Toss halved Brussels sprouts in vegetable oil and lay flat on a baking sheet. Top with slices of dried lemon. Salt and pepper generously. Roast until golden, about 20-30 minutes.

# Mango

*Mango is sweet and delicious, but because of its thick skin and large pit it has the reputation of being hard to handle. The reward for your labor is a fruit that makes any dish taste as if it's been kissed by the sun. With dried mango, you're able to shortcut peeling and pitting the fruit.*

## Ingredients

1 tablespoon fresh lime juice
1 medium ripe mango or 2 cups frozen chopped mango, defrosted

..................................................................................................................................

**1.** Fill a large bowl ¾ full with clean water and add lime juice.

**2.** If using a fresh mango, wash and dry mango. Peel and discard peel. Slice mango flesh from pit.

**3.** Slice fruit ¼" thick. Place mango pieces into bowl of lime juice and water. Let soak 5 minutes.

**4.** Drain mango pieces and spread in a single even layer across one or more dehydrator shelves. Dry at 135°F until reduced in size and dry but still chewy, about 6–8 hours.

**5.** Transfer mango to a clean work surface and cool to room temperature, about 2 hours. Transfer to an airtight container and store.

## Uses

- Mango brings a sweet, sunny quality to tea. Mix 1 tablespoon loose black tea or loose green tea plus 1 slice chopped dried mango in a tea ball or muslin tea bag. Steep as you would regular tea and enjoy!

- Dried mango can take the heat. For a quick sweet and spicy treat, dip dried mango slices in lime juice and sprinkle with crushed dried chili peppers.

- Substitute mango for raisins in your favorite oatmeal cookie recipe and sprinkle with coconut for a change-up from your standard cookie. Just be sure to chop the dried mango to be roughly the same size as raisins.

# Nectarines

*Slightly sweeter and darker than dried peaches and dried apricots, nectarines are a great change of pace when you have a taste for dried stone fruit. They tend to work better in international recipes, whereas dried peaches lend themselves more to American dishes.*

## Ingredients
1 tablespoon fresh lemon juice
1 pound nectarines

..................................................................................................................

**1.** Fill a large bowl ¾ full with clean water and add lemon juice.

**2.** Wash and dry nectarines. Peel and split in half lengthwise. Remove and discard pit. Place nectarine halves into bowl of lemon juice and water.

**3.** Slice each nectarine half into ⅛"-thick slices. Return slices to water and let soak 5 minutes.

**4.** Drain nectarine slices through a wire mesh strainer. Spread in a single even layer across one or more dehydrator shelves. Dry at 135°F until dry to the touch, about 8–10 hours.

**5.** Transfer nectarines to a clean work surface and cool to room temperature, about 2 hours. Transfer to an airtight container and store.

## Uses
- Dried nectarines make a fantastic chutney. Simmer nectarines in water with Indian spices, such as chili peppers, cloves, cinnamon, dried ginger, and black pepper. Remove spices and stir in a little distilled vinegar for a sweet-sour taste. Serve with roasted poultry.
- Swap dried nectarines for raisins or dried apricots in your favorite recipes. When substituting for raisins, make sure you dice the nectarines into small pieces that are roughly the size of raisins.

# Oranges

*In the winter, when oranges are abundant, we can all get our dose of vitamin C. Dried oranges offer the same health benefits, but you can enjoy them all year long. And, unlike fresh oranges, the peel is delicious, so you can eat the whole fruit. Try dehydrating blood oranges using this recipe, which yields a bright red-orange slice that has just a hint of berry flavor.*

## Ingredients

4 large oranges

........................................................................................

**1.** Wash oranges and pat dry. Cut into ¼" slices.

**2.** Spread orange slices in a single even layer across one or more dehydrator shelves. Dry at 135°F until dried orange will snap in half when you bend it, about 11–12 hours.

**3.** Transfer oranges to a clean work surface and cool to room temperature, about 2 hours. Transfer to an airtight container and store.

## Uses

- Dried oranges make gorgeous cocktail garnishes. Float a slice of dried orange across the surface of a martini or cosmopolitan. Or make a quick rimming powder for margaritas. Pulverize dried oranges with equal parts of either salt (for traditional margaritas) or sugar (for sweet margaritas). Place in a small dish. Wet the rim of your cocktail glass, roll in the orange powder, and tap off excess. Fill with your drink.
- Baked fish takes on a delightful Mediterranean flair with the addition of dried oranges. Place thin fish fillets (such as tilapia or sole) onto a baking sheet. Pat dry. Salt and pepper, then lay slices of dried oranges on top of fish. Drizzle with extra-virgin olive oil and bake as usual.
- Make tapenade, a quick appetizer based on olives. Pulse 1 cup pitted black olives (such as kalamata), 1 clove garlic, 1 tablespoon olive oil, a pinch of chili pepper, and 3 slices dried orange in a food processor until you have a slightly chunky mixture. Serve with toast points or crackers.

# Papayas

*The flesh of fresh papaya can vary from light orange to bright pink-orange and dries into a gorgeous dusty rose hue. With flavors of honey and black pepper, its distinct taste is preserved very well by dehydrating, giving you a great option for saving papaya when you've purchased a large fruit and can only eat part of it.*

## Ingredients
1 tablespoon fresh lime juice
1 medium ripe papaya

**1.** Fill a large bowl ¾ full with clean water and add lime juice.

**2.** Wash and dry papaya. Split in half lengthwise. Remove and discard seeds. Peel papaya and slice ¼" thick. Place papaya pieces into bowl of lime juice and water. Let soak 5 minutes.

**3.** Drain papaya pieces and spread in a single even layer across one or more dehydrator shelves. Dry at 135°F until reduced in size and dry, but still chewy, about 6–8 hours.

**4.** Transfer papaya to a clean work surface and cool to room temperature, about 2 hours. Transfer to an airtight container and store.

## Uses
- Coarsely chop dried papaya and add it to store-bought or homemade salsa. The sweetness of the fruit will bring out the flavors of the spice and tomatoes in the salsa. Plus, the vinegar in the salsa will naturally soften the dried papaya.
- Tropical sangria has never been easier. Soak ½ cup dried papaya along with ½ cup of other dried tropical fruits you have on hand (guava, mango, pineapple) in spiced rum overnight. Add to a bottle of dry red wine, along with 2 cups of orange juice and 2 cups of sparkling water. Serve over ice with lime wedges.

# Peaches

*Peaches are a taste of the American South and dried peaches only accentuate that idea. Sweet and tangy, a dried peach will remind you of the best part of a summer-ripe peach.*

### Ingredients
1 tablespoon fresh lemon juice
1 pound peaches

1. Fill a large bowl ¾ full with clean water and add lemon juice.
2. Wash and dry peaches. Peel and split in half lengthwise. Remove and discard pit. Place peach halves into bowl of lemon juice and water.
3. Slice each peach half into ⅛"-thick slices. Return slices to water and let soak 5 minutes.
4. Drain peach slices through a wire mesh strainer. Spread in a single even layer across one or more dehydrator shelves. Dry at 135°F until dry to the touch, about 8–10 hours.
5. Transfer peaches to a clean work surface and cool to room temperature, about 2 hours. Transfer to an airtight container and store.

### Uses
- Make a trail mix with oat granola, dried peaches, and toasted pecans. If desired, add ¼ teaspoon ground cinnamon per cup of trail mix.
- Swap out ¼ of the peaches in your favorite peach cobbler recipe and replace with dried peaches. The liquid from the fresh peaches will rehydrate the dried peaches as the cobbler bakes, and will introduce a new texture to the dessert.
- Butterfly a pork tenderloin. Cover cut side with a thin layer of dried peaches, fresh garlic paste, and crushed chili pepper. Roll tenderloin into a pinwheel and tie with twine. Season with salt and pepper. Roast at 350°F until the center registers 140°F on a meat thermometer, about 35–40 minutes. Allow to rest 5 minutes, and then cut into thin slices.

# Pears

*Dried pears are dried apples' more shapely cousins. Leaving the peels on will not only add a lovely color to these beauties, but will also ensure that the fruit's shape stays intact, and will add vitamins and fiber.*

## Ingredients

1 tablespoon fresh lemon juice

1 pound pears

.......................................................................................................

**1.** Fill a large bowl ¾ full with clean water and add lemon juice.

**2.** If desired, peel pears, discarding peels. Place each peeled pear into the bowl of lemon water.

**3.** Cut each pear in half lengthwise. Using a melon baller, remove seed pack from pear. Return cut pears to water with lemon juice.

**4.** Slice each pear half into ⅛" slices. Return pear slices to water with lemon juice.

**5.** Drain pears through a wire mesh strainer and pat dry with paper towels.

**6.** Spread pear pieces in a single even layer across one or more dehydrator shelves. Dry at 135°F until dried pear will snap in half when you bend it, about 4–6 hours.

**7.** Transfer pears to a clean work surface and cool to room temperature, about 2 hours. Transfer to an airtight container and store.

## Uses

- Decorate the top of quick breads with slices of dried pears. Five minutes prior to the end of baking, arrange dried pears in patterns across the top of a loaf. Return bread to oven and continue to bake until done.

- Replace your everyday crackers with crisp slices of dried pears. Spread with brie, bleu cheese, or goat cheese. Top with a slice of Swiss, Gouda, or Cheddar. Pears work well with most cheese types.

# Plums

*Of all the fruit changed by a dehydrator, plums go through the most dramatic transformation. They go from slightly tart, juicy gems to incredibly sweet and silky dried fruit. A pre-dehydrator soak in honey acts more as a preservative of the fruit, rather than a way of sweetening it.*

## Ingredients
¼ cup honey
1 pound plums

**1.** Fill a large bowl ¾ full with clean water and add honey.
**2.** Wash and dry plums. Split in half lengthwise. Remove and discard pit. Place plum halves into bowl of honey and water. Let soak 2 hours or more.
**3.** Drain plums and spread in a single even layer, cut side down, across one or more dehydrator shelves. Dry at 135°F until reduced in size and dry but still chewy, about 14–16 hours.
**4.** Transfer plums to a clean work surface and cool to room temperature, about 2 hours. Transfer to an airtight container and store.

## Uses
- Prunes accent most roasted vegetables, but work particularly well with veggies that are slightly bitter, like cabbage, cauliflower, Brussels sprouts, or asparagus. Preheat your oven to 325°F. Toss vegetables in oil, salt, and pepper, and add ½ cup of chopped prunes per pound of vegetables. Roast until veggies are golden brown, about 45 minutes. If desired, serve with a little reduced balsamic or pomegranate syrup.
- Add prunes to your favorite stuffing or dressing recipe and serve alongside roasted poultry (it's especially great with duck) or roast pork.

# Pineapples

*A sign of hospitality, pineapple is a great fruit to keep in your house. And what better way to keep it than in its dried form? That way, you can show your hospitality to any guests who arrive without notice. Homemade dried pineapple is also a virtuous treat. Unlike store-bought, the pineapple you dry at home has no added sugar.*

## Ingredients
1 large ripe pineapple

..........................................................................................................................................

**1.** Cut away leaves and skin from pineapple and discard. Remove and discard pineapple's tough inner core. Cut pineapple into ¼" slices.

**2.** Spread pineapple slices in a single even layer across one or more dehydrator shelves. Dry at 125°F until dried pineapple will snap in half when you bend it, about 6–8 hours.

**3.** Transfer pineapple to a clean work surface and cool to room temperature, about 2 hours. Transfer to an airtight container and store.

## Uses
- Substitute dried pineapple in your favorite fruit chutney. The flavor of pineapple pairs well with spices and adds an unexpected flavor. Taste the chutney before adding sugar and vinegar, however, as pineapple may require less sugar and vinegar than other fruits do.
- Dried pineapple is both tangy and sugary at the same time. If you dehydrate pineapple to a crisp stage, you can powder the dried pineapple and use it as a condiment on rich-tasting fish like salmon, sea bass, or cod, or as a sprinkle on grilled pork chops.
- Dried pineapple rings hold their shape better and are less likely to fall apart than fresh or canned pineapple rings. Rehydrate dried pineapple rings to use with a pineapple upside-down cake.

# Quince Paste (Membrillo)

*In Spain, and throughout Latin America, membrillo is a snacking staple. It's a rosy paste with the consistency of soft cheese, made from quince, sugar, and lemon. Although quince is somewhat astringent and extremely hard when raw, quince paste is sweet, tangy, and has a lovely, slightly chewy consistency.*

## Ingredients
2 large quinces
3 tablespoons lemon juice
3 cups sugar

**1.** Wash quinces, peel, and core. Cut into 1" pieces.
**2.** Place quince, lemon juice, and sugar in a large, heavy saucepot. Cover with water by ½". Bring to a boil and reduce heat. Simmer, uncovered, until quince pieces are soft and tender, about 1 hour.
**3.** Transfer mixture to the bowl of a food processor or blender and purée until smooth. Transfer back into pot and return to the stove. Bring to a boil and reduce heat to low. Simmer, stirring frequently, until excess water has evaporated and mixture is deep orange in color, about 90 minutes–1 hour.
**4.** Line a dehydrator rack with parchment paper, foil, or high-heat plastic wrap. Spray with pan spray. Spread quince mixture onto prepared rack in an even layer. Dehydrate at 125°F until firm, about 1–2 hours. Remove quince paste from dehydrator and allow to cool at room temperature 2 hours.
**5.** Cut quince paste into triangles and store in an airtight container in the refrigerator until ready to serve.

## Uses
- Membrillo is often served with dairy products. South Americans enjoy membrillo slices on top of graham crackers that have been spread with cream cheese.
- The sweet-tangy taste makes it a natural foil to medium-bodied meats, such as duck, chicken thighs, or pork roast. Before roasting poultry, loosen skin around the legs and thighs, and tuck in slices of membrillo. Salt and pepper the bird, then roast according to your favorite recipe. For pork, add cubes of it to toasted bread cubes, sautéed leeks, and egg. Slit pork roast and use as stuffing.
- Instead of quince paste, you can make quince jam. Follow this recipe up to the dehydrating part and transfer the quince mixture to canning jars. Cool to room temperature, about 2 hours, and then transfer to your pantry to store. Refrigerate after opening.

# Raisins

*Raisins, of course, are just dried grapes. With varieties of grapes ranging from white to green to red to black, you'd think grocers would offer more varieties of raisins. Not to worry—with a dehydrator, you can make whatever variety of raisins you choose.*

## Ingredients

1 pound seedless grapes

........................................................................................

**1.** Wash grapes and pat dry.

**2.** Spread grapes in a single even layer across one or more dehydrator shelves. Dry at 125°F until raisins reduce in size by ¾ and are dry but still chewy, about 14–18 hours.

**3.** Transfer raisins to a clean work surface and cool to room temperature, about 2 hours. Transfer to an airtight container and store.

## Uses

- Add a handful of golden raisins to your favorite coleslaw recipe. Or make a sweet-savory broccoli slaw with raw broccoli, raisins, sunflower seeds, cooked bacon (if you choose), and a creamy mayonnaise dressing.
- Instead of sugar, honey, or agave nectar, use raisins as a sweetener. Soak raisins in water and purée into a paste. Now you have a sweetener with fiber and vitamins, along with sweetness.
- Add raisins to a grain dish, such as rice pilaf, wild rice, or barley. The sweetness of the raisins will enhance the nutty flavor of the grain and will add an interesting chewy texture.

# Raspberries

*Summer-sweet raspberries are a culinary delight. Fresh raspberries are fragile, however, and last just a few days without molding. To preserve your raspberries while they're at their peak of flavor, dry them. Then use as you would fresh raspberries.*

## Ingredients
1 pint raspberries

..............................................................................................................................

**1.** Wash berries and pat dry.
**2.** Spread berries in a single even layer across one or more dehydrator shelves. Dry at 125°F until berries crush easily between your fingertips, about 12–14 hours.
**3.** Transfer raspberries to a clean work surface and cool to room temperature, about 2 hours. Transfer to an airtight container and store.

## Uses

- Make natural pink lemonade by pulverizing dried raspberries and adding to your favorite lemonade recipe. The tartness of the lemons will accentuate the raspberry flavor, and the raspberries will give the lemonade a healthy blush.
- Rehydrate raspberries in red wine or ruby port, drain, and use as a topping for baked brie. Place a wheel of brie onto the center of a sheet of puff pastry. Top with rehydrated raspberries, and draw the puff pastry up around the brie. Crimp edges to close. Brush with egg wash. Bake at 400°F until golden brown, about 20 minutes.
- Mix dried raspberries in with fresh raspberries, blackberries, or blueberries in your favorite pie or cobbler recipe.

# Strawberries

*One bite of a crisp dehydrated strawberry and you may forget that you also love the taste of fresh strawberries. The berry flavor and sweetness intensify during dehydration, making even off-season berries a sweet delight.*

**Ingredients**

1 quart strawberries

...................................................................................................................................................

**1.** Wash berries and pat dry. Remove and discard stems. Slice berries ⅛" thick.

**2.** Spread berries in a single even layer across one or more dehydrator shelves. Dry at 125°F until berries crush easily between your fingertips, about 6–8 hours.

**3.** Transfer strawberries to a clean work surface and cool to room temperature, about 2 hours. Transfer to an airtight container and store.

**Uses**

- Instead of bacon, use dried strawberries as a garnish for spinach salads. Top with your favorite Russian dressing, chopped eggs, and sunflower seeds to make a satisfying and sweet protein-packed lunch.

- Decorate the top and sides of frosted cakes with dried strawberries. They have the same color and shape as fresh strawberries, and therefore will create the same visual effect. But because they're dried, they will not release their liquid onto the top of a cake, therefore keeping the dessert fresher-looking.

- In need of a quick dessert for unexpected company? Top slices of store-bought pound cake with dried strawberries that have rehydrated in triple sec for 20 minutes. Add a dollop of whipped cream or a scoop of vanilla ice cream.

# Tangerines

*A slightly more honeyed version of oranges, tangerines also make excellent dried fruit. Their natural sweetness intensifies during the drying process and makes them a terrific on-the-go snack option. They also work well in entrées, side dishes, salads, and desserts.*

## Ingredients

5–6 tangerines or clementines

.......................................................................................................................

**1.** Wash tangerines and pat dry. Cut into ¼" slices.
**2.** Spread tangerines in a single even layer across one or more dehydrator shelves. Dry at 135°F until dried tangerine will snap in half when you bend it, about 6–7 hours.
**3.** Transfer tangerines to a clean work surface and cool to room temperature, about 2 hours. Transfer to an airtight container and store.

## Uses

- Instead of the usual orange, substitute dried tangerine in your favorite cranberry-orange bread or muffin recipe. The extra sweetness imparted by the tangerines will soften the cranberry's tart properties even better than oranges do.
- Add a dash of color, crunch, and sweetness to pickled beets. Roast a bunch of beets until tender, peel, and cube (or buy canned cooked beets). Add 3-4 dried tangerine slices, ¼ cup sliced white onions, and 1 teaspoon dried dill. Place into jars, cover with distilled white vinegar and store in the refrigerator until ready to use.
- Crumble dried tangerines over your next stir-fry to perk up the flavors and introduce a satisfying crunch.
- Steep a slice of tangerine in your next cup of hot cocoa for 5 minutes, then remove and discard. The citrus splash really wakes up the chocolate flavor, and cuts through some of the richness.

# CHAPTER 6
# Meats and Fish

While store-bought beef jerky may be a tasty, satisfying snack, homemade beef jerky blows it away. You can control the sodium and spice level, as well as dry it to your preferred texture. Homemade beef jerky is made without preservatives or anti-caking agents, so you know it's wholesome. This first recipe is for basic Beef Jerky (subsequent recipes give you ideas on how to change the flavorings in your jerky). You may also use venison or lamb in this recipe.

Unlike other dried foods in this book, these flavorful jerkies are stand-alone recipes. Flavored dried meats don't lend themselves well to recipes.

# Beef Jerky

*A backpacker's staple, this simple beef jerky is a quick way to preserve meat to use when camping, hiking, or even when you're looking for a protein-packed snack. Flank steak, a naturally lean cut of meat, makes this jerky a healthy bite that has significantly less fat than some commercially prepared jerkies.*

## Ingredients

2 pounds flank steak

1 cup Worcestershire sauce

1 teaspoon ground dried garlic

¼ cup dried onions

½ teaspoon dried chili powder

½ teaspoon ground black pepper

**1.** Place flank steak in a zipper bag (or wrap in plastic wrap) and freeze for 2 hours. This makes it easier for you to cut the steak.

**2.** While steak freezes, mix remaining ingredients in a medium bowl.

**3.** Remove steak from freezer and slice with the grain into long, narrow strips. Each strip should be ¼" thick by 1"–2" wide (which is about the height of the steak) by 3"–4" long.

**4.** Toss steak into the marinade and cover the bowl. Marinate in your refrigerator 6–8 hours, or overnight.

**5.** Line three dehydrator racks completely with plastic wrap. Brush with vegetable oil or spray with pan spray. Remove each steak strip from marinade using tongs. Shake over bowl to remove excess marinade and place in a single layer on rack. Repeat with remaining steak strips.

**6.** Place racks into dehydrator and set to 145°F.

**7.** Check steak after 8 hours. Jerky is ready when it's dry to the touch, and snaps when bent. If jerky is not dry, check again in an hour. Depending on the thickness of your strips, the circulation of your dehydrator, and the amount of marinade you were able to remove from the jerky, it may take up to 12 hours to dry.

**8.** Once jerky is dry, remove rack from dehydrator and allow to cool to room temperature, about 2 hours. Transfer to an airtight container and store.

# Jerk-Spiced Jerky

*Jamaican jerk seasoning is a great way to spice up your jerky. It combines the tang of lime juice with island spices such as allspice and nutmeg, and introduces a hint of heat from Thai or jalapeño peppers. This recipe lets you use some of the dried ingredients you have on hand, such as dried thyme, dried scallions, dried chives, and dried garlic powder.*

## Ingredients

2 pounds flank steak

1 cup fresh lime juice

1 cup soy sauce

1 teaspoon ground nutmeg

2 teaspoons ground cinnamon

½ teaspoon ground allspice

½ teaspoon ground cloves

1 teaspoon ground coriander

½ teaspoon ground black pepper

1 whole dried green chili pepper (such as Thai pepper or jalapeño)

½ teaspoon dried thyme

¼ cup dark brown sugar, packed

¼ cup dried scallions

¼ cup dried chives

1 tablespoon dried garlic powder

........................................................................................

**1.** Place flank steak in a zipper bag (or wrap in plastic wrap) and freeze for 2 hours. This makes it easier for you to cut the steak.

**2.** While steak freezes, mix remaining ingredients in a medium bowl.

**3.** Remove steak from freezer and slice with the grain into long, narrow strips. Each strip should be ¼" thick by 1"–2" wide (which is about the height of the steak) by 3"–4" long.

**4.** Toss steak into the marinade and cover the bowl. Marinate in your refrigerator 6–8 hours, or overnight.

**5.** Line three dehydrator racks completely with plastic wrap. Brush with vegetable oil or spray with pan spray. Remove each steak strip from marinade using tongs. Shake over bowl to remove excess marinade and place in a single layer on rack. Repeat with remaining steak strips.

**6.** Place racks into dehydrator and set to 145°F.

**7.** Check steak after 8 hours. Jerky is ready when it's dry to the touch, and snaps when bent. If jerky is not dry, check again in an hour. Depending on the thickness of your strips, the circulation of your dehydrator, and the amount of marinade you were able to remove from the jerky, it may take up to 12 hours to dry.

**8.** Once jerky is dry, remove rack from dehydrator and allow to cool to room temperature, about 2 hours. Transfer to an airtight container and store.

# Mexican-Spiced Jerky

*A combination of tomatoes, lime, chili, cumin, and oregano is hard to beat in this jerky inspired by south-of-the-border ingredients. Take this on your next camping trip to spice up a hike. Just make sure you also pack plenty of water.*

## Ingredients

2 pounds flank steak

1 cup tomato purée

Juice from 1 lime (about 2 tablespoons)

2 tablespoons salt

1 teaspoon ground dried garlic

1 teaspoon dried chili powder

1 teaspoon ground cumin

½ teaspoon dried oregano

.......................................................................................................................................

**1.** Place flank steak in a zipper bag (or wrap in plastic wrap) and freeze for 2 hours. This makes it easier for you to cut the steak.

**2.** While steak freezes, mix remaining ingredients in a medium bowl.

**3.** Remove steak from freezer and slice with the grain into long, narrow strips. Each strip should be ¼" thick by 1"–2" wide (which is about the height of the steak) by 3"–4" long.

**4.** Toss steak into the marinade and cover the bowl. Marinate in your refrigerator 6–8 hours, or overnight.

**5.** Line three dehydrator racks completely with plastic wrap. Brush with vegetable oil or spray with pan spray. Remove each steak strip from marinade using tongs. Shake over bowl to remove excess marinade and place in a single layer on rack. Repeat with remaining steak strips.

**6.** Place racks into dehydrator and set to 145°F.

**7.** Check steak after 8 hours. Jerky is ready when it's dry to the touch, and snaps when bent. If jerky is not dry, check again in an hour. Depending on the thickness of your strips, the circulation of your dehydrator, and the amount of marinade you were able to remove from the jerky, it may take up to 12 hours to dry.

**8.** Once jerky is dry, remove rack from dehydrator and allow to cool to room temperature, about 2 hours. Transfer to an airtight container and store.

# Teriyaki Beef Jerky

*Soy sauce is a great base flavor for making jerky. It's rich and slightly salty, and works to preserve the meat. You can make a jerky with a nice dose of soy sauce, along with Asian flavorings. This recipe works well for buffalo or venison as well as beef.*

## Ingredients

2 pounds flank steak

2 cups soy sauce or tamari

1 cup honey

¼ cup sherry or rice wine

1 tablespoon fresh garlic, minced

1 teaspoon ground dried ginger

**1.** Place flank steak in a zipper bag (or wrap in plastic wrap) and freeze for 2 hours. This makes it easier for you to cut the steak.

**2.** While steak freezes, mix remaining ingredients in a medium bowl.

**3.** Remove steak from freezer and slice with the grain into long, narrow strips. Each strip should be ¼" thick by 1"–2" wide (which is about the height of the steak) by 3"–4" long.

**4.** Toss steak into the marinade and cover the bowl. Marinate in your refrigerator 6–8 hours, or overnight.

**5.** Line three dehydrator racks completely with plastic wrap. Brush with vegetable oil or spray with pan spray. Remove each steak strip from marinade using tongs. Shake over bowl to remove excess marinade and place in a single layer on rack. Repeat with remaining steak strips.

**6.** Place racks into dehydrator and set to 145°F.

**7.** Check steak after 8 hours. Jerky is ready when it's dry to the touch, and snaps when bent. If jerky is not dry, check again in an hour. Depending on the thickness of your strips, the circulation of your dehydrator, and the amount of marinade you were able to remove from the jerky, it may take up to 12 hours to dry.

**8.** Once jerky is dry, remove rack from dehydrator and allow to cool to room temperature, about 2 hours. Transfer to an airtight container and store.

# Chicken Jerky

*For those who don't eat red meat (or would like a break from traditional beef jerky), poultry is a great alternative. This recipe gives you a starting point for making jerky from boneless, skinless chicken breasts. You can substitute turkey for chicken in this recipe, if you prefer.*

## Ingredients

2 pounds boneless, skinless chicken breasts

2 quarts water

1 cup salt

¼ cup brown sugar

1 teaspoon garlic powder

1 teaspoon paprika

2 dried bay leaves, crushed

¼ teaspoon dried hot chili powder

**1.** Place chicken in a zipper bag (or wrap in plastic wrap) and freeze for 1 hour. This makes it easier for you to cut.

**2.** While chicken freezes, mix remaining ingredients in a medium bowl.

**3.** Remove chicken from freezer and slice with the grain into long, narrow strips. Each strip should be ¼" thick by 1"–2" wide (which is about the height of the chicken) by 3"–4" long.

**4.** Toss chicken into the marinade and cover the bowl. Marinate in your refrigerator 1–2 hours.

**5.** Line three dehydrator racks completely with plastic wrap. Brush with vegetable oil or spray with pan spray. Remove each chicken strip from marinade using tongs. Shake over bowl to remove excess marinade and place in a single layer on rack. Repeat with remaining chicken strips.

**6.** Place racks into dehydrator and set to 145°F.

**7.** Check chicken after 4 hours. Jerky is ready when it's dry to the touch, and snaps when bent. If jerky is not dry, check again in an hour. Depending on the thickness of your strips, the circulation of your dehydrator, and the amount of marinade you were able to remove from the jerky, it may take up to 8 hours to dry.

**8.** Once jerky is dry, remove rack from dehydrator and allow to cool to room temperature, about 2 hours. Transfer to an airtight container and store.

# Turkey Jerky

*This jerky tastes a little like Thanksgiving dinner, with its combination of traditional holiday spices such as sage and rosemary. It's made with a hint of sweetness, which brings out the rich flavor of turkey. You may also make this recipe with boneless skinless chicken breasts.*

## Ingredients

1 half turkey breast, boneless

2 quarts water

1 cup salt

¼ cup brown sugar

1 teaspoon garlic powder

1 teaspoon dried sage

1 teaspoon dried rosemary

1 teaspoon dried thyme

1. Place turkey in a zipper bag (or wrap in plastic wrap) and freeze for 2 hours. This makes it easier for you to cut.
2. While turkey freezes, mix remaining ingredients in a medium bowl.
3. Remove turkey from freezer and slice with the grain into long, narrow strips. Each strip should be ¼" thick by 1"–2" wide (which is about the height of the turkey breast) by 3"–4" long.
4. Toss turkey into the marinade and cover the bowl. Marinate in your refrigerator 3–4 hours.
5. Line 3 dehydrator racks completely with plastic wrap. Brush with vegetable oil or spray with pan spray. Remove each turkey strip from marinade using tongs. Shake over bowl to remove excess marinade and place in a single layer on rack. Repeat with remaining turkey strips.
6. Place racks into dehydrator and set to 145°F.
7. Check turkey after 4 hours. Jerky is ready when it's dry to the touch, and snaps when bent. If jerky is not dry, check again in an hour. Depending on the thickness of your strips, the circulation of your dehydrator, and the amount of marinade you were able to remove from the jerky, it may take up to 8 hours to dry.
8. Once jerky is dry, remove rack from dehydrator and allow to cool to room temperature, about 2 hours. Transfer to an airtight container and store.

# Dried Cod

*Dried salt cod is a dietary staple in Spain, France, and Italy, where it is often rehydrated at Christmas for a special holiday treat. Here, you can make your own dried cod whenever you find that you've got an extra "catch" on hand.*

## Ingredients
1 pound boneless, skinless cod fillets
1 roll paper towels
1 cup salt

**1.** Place cod on a clean work surface and blot all over with paper towels, pressing to remove excess moisture.
**2.** Place half of salt into a shallow dish. Add cod and pour remaining salt over cod. Wrap in a double layer of paper towels, place on a rack over a baking sheet, and allow to dry 2 hours in your refrigerator.
**3.** Remove cod from refrigerator, unwrap, and discard paper towel.
**4.** Transfer cod to a dehydrator shelf. Dehydrate at 145°F until dry to the touch, about 6–8 hours.
**5.** Once cod is dry, remove rack from dehydrator and allow to cool to room temperature, about 2 hours. Transfer to an airtight container and store. Because this recipe is simply cod and salt, dried cod can be used quite nicely in recipes.

## Uses
- Make a quick fish stock by soaking salt cod in a container of fresh water in the refrigerator for eight hours. Drain and rinse, then place cod into a saucepot, cover with water, and add carrots, onions, celery, and a bay leaf. Simmer 2 hours and drain. The resulting stock can be used as a base for fish soups, clam chowder, or lobster bisque.
- Flake dried salt cod into equal parts of sour cream and mayonnaise, or into a block of cream cheese, for a quick seafood spread.

# Salmon Jerky

*This lean, protein-packed snack is also loaded with healthy omega-3 fatty acids, making it the perfect snack after a workout. The light marinade works well with the rich flavor of the salmon. If you prefer, you may instead use the marinade used in the teriyaki beef jerky for salmon.*

## Ingredients

1¼ pounds skin-on salmon

½ cup soy sauce

1 tablespoon light brown sugar

1 tablespoon fresh lime juice

1 teaspoon black pepper

1 pinch dried hot chili powder

.........................................................................................................................................................

**1.** Place salmon, skin side down, on a clean work surface. Run your hand against the grain of the fish, feeling for bones. Using tweezers or fish pliers, remove all bones.

**2.** Transfer salmon to a zipper bag (or wrap in plastic wrap) and freeze for 1 hour. This makes it easier for you to cut.

**3.** While salmon freezes, mix remaining ingredients in a medium bowl.

**4.** Remove salmon from freezer and slice with the grain into long, narrow strips. Each strip should be ¼" thick by 1"–2" wide by 3"–4" long.

**5.** Toss salmon into the marinade and cover the bowl. Marinate in your refrigerator for 1½–3 hours.

**6.** Line three dehydrator racks completely with plastic wrap. Brush with vegetable oil or spray with pan spray. Remove each salmon strip from marinade using tongs. Shake over bowl to remove excess marinade and place in a single layer on rack. Repeat with remaining salmon strips.

**7.** Place racks into dehydrator and set to 145°F.

**8.** Check salmon after 3 hours. Jerky is ready when it's dry to the touch, and snaps when bent. If jerky is not dry, check again in an hour. Depending on the thickness of your strips, the circulation of your dehydrator, and the amount of marinade you were able to remove from the jerky, it may take up to 8 hours to dry.

**9.** Once jerky is dry, remove rack from dehydrator and allow jerky to cool to room temperature, about 2 hours. Transfer to an airtight container and store.

# Scallops

*Throughout Asia, dried shellfish is used to add a savory, meaty flavor to dishes. Drying scallops was a traditional way to preserve excess seafood after a large scallop harvest. Now, modern Asian cuisine uses dried scallops, also known as conpoy, as a luxury ingredient. You can dry scallops at home, saving you a trip to your local specialty grocer.*

## Ingredients
1 pound raw scallops, each scallop's "foot" removed
1 roll paper towels
1 teaspoon salt

........................................................................................

**1.** Split each scallop in half lengthwise. Pat scallop halves dry with paper towel and sprinkle evenly with salt.

**2.** Spread scallops in a single even layer, cut side up, across one or more dehydrator shelves. Dehydrate at 145°F until dry to the touch and very firm, about 8–10 hours.

**3.** Transfer scallops to a clean work surface and cool to room temperature, about 2 hours. Transfer to an airtight container and store.

## Uses
- Rehydrate scallops with steam or simmering water for 1–2 hours. Drain, pat dry, and roughly chop.
- Use rehydrated conpoy in a mixed seafood salad with other shellfish such as shrimp and squid. Make a tangy lime dressing with just a touch of hot sauce.
- Add dried scallops to sautéed green vegetables, such as broccoli or bok choy.

# Shrimp

*Dried shrimp are used in coastal regions around the world to add both salt and umami (a savory/meaty taste) to dishes. They are commonly used throughout Asia, in Western Africa, and in Brazil, where they flavor anything from sautéed vegetables to tomato broth to rice dishes.*

## Ingredients
1 tablespoon salt
1 pound raw shrimp, peeled, deveined, and tails removed

**1.** Bring a large pot of water to a rolling boil. Add salt and bring back to a boil. Add shrimp and cook, uncovered, until shrimp is bright pink, about 3 minutes.

**2.** Drain shrimp and plunge into ice water to chill. Drain and blot with paper towels.

**3.** Split each shrimp in half lengthwise.

**4.** Spread shrimp in a single even layer, cut side up, across one or more dehydrator shelves. Dehydrate at 145°F until dry to the touch and very firm, about 3–5 hours.

**5.** Transfer shrimp to a clean work surface and cool to room temperature, about 2 hours. Transfer to an airtight container and store.

## Uses
- Dried shrimp make a great addition to your favorite fried rice recipe. Rehydrate shrimp, drain, and chop finely. Then add as the final ingredient before serving.
- Make homemade Cantonese XO sauce with dried shrimp. Combine ½ cup dried shrimp, ¼ cup dried hot chili peppers, 1 tablespoon dried garlic, and 1 cup vegetable oil (such as canola oil or safflower oil) in a blender. Purée until smooth. Use as a condiment to add spice, salt, and umami to stir-fried dishes.
- You can pulverize dried shrimp using a food processor. Once you powder shrimp, use it to boost the flavor of seafood gumbo or shrimp bisque, or as a condiment that adds both a salty and shrimplike flavor.

### That Annoying Fish Smell
Some foods while they're dehydrating spread wonderful smells around your house, but some don't. Fish fits into that latter category. If you don't want your house smelling like you've been cooking fish for weeks on end, crank open a window before you start dehydrating.

# CHAPTER 7
# Herbs and Dairy

One of the bright spots in any garden is a section of herbs growing in a sunny patch. With a quick trip out to this part of your garden, you can add freshness and flavor to any dish. As most gardeners know, it's challenging to use all your fresh herbs before the growing season is done. Enter drying! Your own dehydrated herbs pack much more flavor than the store-bought herbs—plus you never feel like you've got to let your garden's bounty go to waste.

What applies to herbs also applies to dairy. So often, you'll have a drawer full of half-eaten cheeses. By dehydrating and then pulverizing cheese, you get cheese powder, which lasts much longer than cheese, and is a great staple for sprinkling on snack foods or adding to soups and stews.

# Basil

*When basil is in season, there is a wealth of delicious and summery dishes that rely on this Mediterranean staple—from pesto to insalata caprese. However, as the weather cools, fresh basil becomes scarce and expensive. To keep the flavor of summer around all year long, save a bit of your crop of fresh basil and dehydrate it. You'll find the taste to be fresher than your typical store-bought dried basil.*

### Ingredients
1 bunch basil

**1.** Wash basil and pat dry. Remove stems and discard. Spread basil leaves in a single even layer across one or more dehydrator shelves. Dry at 135°F until basil leaves crumble easily when rubbed between fingertips, about 90 minutes–3 hours.

**2.** Transfer basil to a clean work surface and cool to room temperature, about 2 hours. Transfer to an airtight container and store.

### Uses
- Basil isn't just for Italian dishes; you will also find it in Southeast Asia, in the cuisines of Thailand and Vietnam. Dry an Asian variety of basil, such as Thai basil or opal basil, to use when you make dishes such as Thai curries or spicy Vietnamese broths.
- Basil adds an herbaceous kick to cocktails when it's in a simple syrup. Heat 1 cup of sugar with 1 cup of water until it's completely dissolved. Add 2 tablespoons dried basil and steep 20 minutes or longer. Strain and keep in a jar in the refrigerator. Use in place of simple syrup in drinks such as Tom Collins or Mojitos.

# Bay Leaves

*Bay leaves grow in temperate climates, such as the west coast of the United States and the Mediterranean, and fresh bay leaves are a terrific addition to soups and stews. However, when bay leaves are at the peak of their flavor in late September to early November, you'll find that you can't use them quickly enough. Because they are so strong in flavor, more than a single bay leaf or two will overpower a dish. Luckily, they are terrific dried, and are welcome in most dishes.*

### Ingredients
20 fresh bay leaves

......................................................................................................

**1.** Wash bay leaves and pat dry. Trim stems to be flush with bottom of bay leaves and discard stems. Spread bay leaves in a single even layer across one or more dehydrator shelves. Dry at 135°F until bay leaves crumble easily when rubbed between fingertips, about 90 minutes–3 hours.

**2.** Transfer bay leaves to a clean work surface and cool to room temperature, about 2 hours. Transfer to an airtight container and store.

### Uses

- Bay leaves are essential to a bouquet garni, which is a package of herbs used to flavor soups, stews, and stocks. To create a bouquet garni, place 1 dried bay leaf, 5–6 black peppercorns, 1 teaspoon dried parsley, and 1 teaspoon dried thyme into cheesecloth and secure with twine. Add to your stock or soup and remove before serving.

- You can also use dried bay leaves for decorative purposes. They are a welcome addition to most potpourri mixes, and also make nice wreaths when you find you have an abundance.

# Chives

*Long and lanky, chives are an herb that is as beautiful as it is functional. Fresh chives are often used as an edible tie for bundles of vegetables. Chives degrade quickly after picking, however, losing both their texture and their taste. Dehydrating is an ideal method for preserving chives. Not only will you retain their delicate flavor, but you also have a ready-made garnish.*

## Ingredients

1 bunch chives

...........................................................................................................................................

**1.** Wash chives and pat dry. Line a dehydrator shelf with foil, parchment paper, or plastic wrap. Using scissors, snip chives into ¼" lengths.

**2.** Spread chives in a single even layer across prepared dehydrator shelf. Dry at 135°F until chives crumble easily when rubbed between fingertips, about 90 minutes–3 hours.

**3.** Transfer chives to a clean work surface and cool to room temperature, about 2 hours. Transfer to an airtight container and store.

## Uses

• Dried chives make a ready substitute for fresh chives on baked potatoes. Simply shake dried chives onto a hot potato, allowing the steam and melted butter to soften the dried chives.

• The next time you're making biscuits, add a tablespoon of dried chives, along with ½ cup of grated Cheddar cheese, to your favorite recipe. Bake as usual. The combination makes even packaged biscuit mix taste homemade.

• Chives are terrific with fish, and a great way to prepare fish is *en papillote* ("in paper") with chives. Place a raw fish fillet onto half of a piece of aluminum foil. Sprinkle with salt, pepper, and chives. Fold the other half over onto the fish and crimp foil to seal tightly. Bake at 400°F until cooked through, about 7 minutes for thin fish fillets like tilapia, and 10–12 minutes for thicker fish such as salmon or sea bass.

# Dill

*Feathery dill is a lovely herb that adds a subtle taste to vegetables, fish, and white meat chicken. It's also an essential part of dill pickles. Dill's thin needles hold up well in the dehydrator and dried dill is every bit as welcome in recipes as fresh dill is.*

## Ingredients
1 bunch dill

**1.** Wash dill and pat dry. Remove stems and discard. Line a dehydrator shelf with foil, parchment paper, or plastic wrap.

**2.** Spread dill in a single even layer across prepared dehydrator shelf. Dry at 125°F until dill crumbles easily when rubbed between fingertips, about 90 minutes–3 hours.

**3.** Transfer dill to a clean work surface and cool to room temperature, about 2 hours. Transfer to an airtight container and store.

## Uses
- Make quick pickles: Cut small cucumbers lengthwise into spears. Place in canning jars with 1 tablespoon kosher salt, 1 teaspoon dried dill, and 2–3 allspice berries. Bring distilled white vinegar to a boil and pour over cucumbers, making sure you cover cucumbers by at least ½". Allow to cool to room temperature, about 2 hours. Cover and refrigerate. Eat when chilled.
- Sprinkle dill liberally over fish before baking. If desired, add dried or fresh lemon, along with salt and pepper.
- Add dried dill to your favorite creamy chicken salad recipe. Dill accentuates mayonnaise, yogurt, or sour cream-based dressings for chicken. And if you'd like a little sweetness, add a handful of dried cranberries. Cranberry and dill is an unexpectedly good flavor combination.

# Mint

*Cooks love mint because it works well in both sweet and savory dishes. In addition, you can always find a mint variety that matches your taste, as there are scores of mint types—ranging from standards like peppermint and spearmint, to unusual varieties such as chocolate mint or pineapple mint. While dried mint is readily available at stores, for freshness and quality nothing beats mint you dehydrate yourself.*

### Ingredients

1 bunch mint

................................................................................

**1.** Wash mint and pat dry. Remove stems and discard.

**2.** Spread mint leaves in a single even layer across one or more dehydrator shelves. Dry at 135°F until mint leaves crumble easily when rubbed between fingertips, about 90 minutes–3 hours.

**3.** Transfer mint to a clean work surface and cool to room temperature, about 2 hours. Transfer to an airtight container and store.

### Uses

- Because there are different types of mint, try dehydrating different varieties and testing them out in your recipes. Pineapple mint is delicious on roast chicken and Middle Eastern varieties of mint, such as Moroccan or Egyptian mint, give tabbouleh an authentic taste. Keep dried mint types in separate jars and label so that you know which mint you've used in a recipe.
- Mint is a natural for lamb. Mix 1 tablespoon dried mint, 1 teaspoon dried garlic powder, ½ teaspoon black pepper, and 2 tablespoons olive oil, and place in a zipper bag. Add 4 lamb chops and marinate 4-6 hours, or even overnight. Remove from marinade, pat dry, season with salt, and either grill or broil.
- Sprinkle dried mint on your next fruit salad. The mint will make many fruits taste sweeter and will add an elegant touch.

# Oregano

*Oregano is a member of the mint family, and can taste similar to mint. Like mint, it pairs well with lighter meats, such as chicken or fish, but it also tastes wonderful on red meats such as beef or lamb. Drying your own ensures that you have the boldest-tasting oregano, which will make your recipes sing.*

## Ingredients

1 bunch oregano

**1.** Wash oregano and pat dry. Remove stems and discard.

**2.** Spread oregano in a single even layer across one or more dehydrator shelves. Dry at 135°F until oregano crumbles easily when rubbed between fingertips, about 90 minutes–3 hours.

**3.** Transfer oregano to a clean work surface and cool to room temperature, about 2 hours. Transfer to an airtight container and store.

## Uses

- Spice up bottled pizza sauce with an addition of oregano. Heat your favorite sauce and add 1 teaspoon dried oregano. Simmer 10 minutes to let flavor meld and use to top pizza. Alternately, if you don't have time to simmer sauce, sprinkle dried oregano on the exposed crust of pizza and bake.
- Oregano is used extensively in Mexico, often with cumin. To make your own ground beef for tacos, brown 1 pound ground beef with 1 tablespoon cumin, 1 teaspoon dried oregano, and 1 teaspoon garlic powder, stirring often. When beef is cooked through, add 2 tablespoons tomato paste and season to taste.
- Take prepared hummus to the next level. Stir a teaspoon of dried oregano into a cup of hummus to give it true Middle Eastern flair.

# Parsley

*As a result of the size of parsley bunches sold in stores, you're bound to have leftover parsley from time to time, and dehydrating is a great way to save the herb. And unlike store-bought dried parsley, which contains leaves and stems, you can ensure that your parsley contains leaves only, giving it a stronger flavor.*

## Ingredients

1 bunch parsley

**1.** Wash parsley and pat dry. Remove stems and reserve for another use, such as stock.

**2.** Spread parsley in a single even layer across one or more dehydrator shelves. Dry at 135°F until parsley crumbles easily when rubbed between fingertips, about 90 minutes–3 hours.

**3.** Transfer parsley to a clean work surface and cool to room temperature, about 2 hours. Transfer to an airtight container and store.

## Uses

- Use as a substitute for fresh parsley in recipes. For each tablespoon of fresh parsley, use 1 teaspoon dried parsley.
- Mix dried parsley in equal parts with dried thyme, oregano, and basil to make an herb blend for chicken or fish.
- Roll soft cheese in parsley to make it decorative enough to serve to guests.

# Rosemary

*With needle-like leaves and woody stems, rosemary dehydrates nicely. In fact, the taste of dried rosemary is closer to fresh rosemary than any other dried herb is to its fresh counterpart. Drying concentrates the pine scent of the leaves, making them ready to transform any dish with just a little sprinkle.*

## Ingredients

1 bunch rosemary

**1.** Wash rosemary and pat dry. Remove stems and discard or reserve for another use.

**2.** Spread rosemary in a single even layer across one or more dehydrator shelves. Dry at 135°F until rosemary crumbles easily when rubbed between fingertips, about 90 minutes–3 hours.

**3.** Transfer rosemary to a clean work surface and cool to room temperature, about 2 hours. Transfer to an airtight container and store.

## Uses

- For a twist on traditional cranberry sauce, stir 1 teaspoon dried rosemary into 2 cups of homemade or store-bought cranberry sauce. This combination pairs well with poultry and is a nice sandwich spread for turkey or chicken sandwiches.
- Rosemary accents pork beautifully. Sprinkle dried rosemary and garlic over your next pork roast, or add dried rosemary to your favorite stuffing for stuffed pork chops.
- Instead of discarding rosemary stems, use them as skewers for appetizers of shrimp, chicken, or beef. Dry stems will need to be soaked before grilling (or they will burn), but fresh rosemary stems do not require soaking.

### A Light Hand with the Rosemary

Rosemary is known as a dominant herb, meaning a little goes a long way. Get too heavy-handed and you can ruin a dish. Be extra careful with the dried variety too. The standard conversion for herbs is, 1 tablespoon fresh equals 1 teaspoon dried. However with rosemary, add a pinch, taste test, and then slowly add more as necessary.

# Sage

*Drying sage takes long silvery leaves and turns them into a lovely silver-green powder that is recipe-ready. Because sage naturally contains so much essential oil, most recipes need just a pinch to create a flavor boost.*

**Ingredients**

2 bunches sage

.................................................................................................

**1.** Wash sage and pat dry. Trim stems to be flush with bottom of sage leaves and discard stems.

**2.** Spread sage in a single even layer across one or more dehydrator shelves. Dry at 135°F until sage crumbles easily when rubbed between fingertips, about 90 minutes–3 hours.

**3.** Transfer sage to a clean work surface and cool to room temperature, about 2 hours. Transfer to an airtight container and store.

**Uses**

- Sage adds a nice taste dimension to sweet vegetables, such as sweet potatoes, carrots, parsnips, or winter squash. Stir a pinch of dried sage into butternut squash soup. Sauté dried sage in butter to use as a topping for pumpkin risotto. Roast with carrots. Or mash into cooked sweet potatoes.
- Mushrooms and other earthy-flavored ingredients also benefit from dried sage. When grilling Portobello mushrooms, marinate in balsamic vinegar, dried sage, and olive oil for a half hour. Remove from marinade, pat dry, and grill as usual.
- Turn bottled Alfredo sauce into a sage sauce for chicken with the addition of sage. Add ½ teaspoon dried sage per cup of sauce. Heat and serve over sautéed chicken.

# Tarragon

*Tarragon is at home in any kitchen. It boasts a light anise-like flavor, which lends itself to lighter fare like vegetables and white meats. By drying tarragon, you ensure that you can add this delicate flavor to your dishes at a moment's notice.*

## Ingredients

1 bunch tarragon

**1.** Wash tarragon and pat dry.

**2.** Spread in a single even layer across one or more dehydrator shelves. Dry at 125°F until leaves crumble easily when rubbed between fingertips, about 1–2 hours.

**3.** Transfer tarragon to a clean work surface and cool to room temperature, about 2 hours. Using clean, dry hands, remove tarragon leaves from stems. Transfer leaves to an airtight container and store.

## Uses

- Potato hash takes on a fresher taste with a little dried tarragon. Toward the end of cooking, sprinkle hash with a little dried tarragon and cook until the potatoes are crispy. The flavor of tarragon accentuates both white potatoes and sweet potatoes.
- Make a tarragon–summer squash casserole. Layer thin slices of zucchini and yellow squash with tomato sauce and dried tarragon. Cover with Parmesan cheese and bake at 350°F until bubbly and set, about 30 minutes. Let rest 10 minutes before slicing.
- Generously coat a side of salmon with tarragon, add oil, salt, and pepper, and roast until salmon flakes easily.

# Thyme

*One of the most-used herbs, thyme finds itself at home in basic soups, on vegetables, and on both fish and meat. Dried thyme is very similar to fresh thyme, and can be used as a substitute for fresh thyme in recipes.*

## Ingredients

1 bunch thyme

**1.** Wash thyme and pat dry.

**2.** Spread in a single even layer across one or more dehydrator shelves. Dry at 125°F until thyme leaves crumble easily when rubbed between fingertips, about 1–2 hours.

**3.** Transfer thyme to a clean work surface and cool to room temperature, about 2 hours. Using clean, dry hands, remove thyme leaves from stems. Transfer leaves to an airtight container and store.

## Uses

- Add a teaspoon of dried thyme and a squeeze of lemon juice (or a sprinkling of crushed dried lemon) to fresh berries to create a berry salad. Serve with a dollop of lightly sweetened whipped cream.

- Cook mushrooms with dried thyme. Either rehydrate and drain dried mushrooms or slice fresh mushrooms. Sauté in butter until golden brown and excess liquid is cooked away. Add ½ teaspoon dried thyme and ¼ cup red or white wine. Cook until wine has evaporated, about 5 minutes. Season to taste with salt and pepper.

- Create a simple side dish: Cut onions into quarters, leaving on skin. Toss in oil with salt, pepper, and dried thyme. Roast at 350°F until onion is soft and golden, about 45 minutes. Remove papery skin, and drizzle with balsamic vinegar.

# Lavender

*Bright purple and heavily perfumed, lavender is a delightful flower that, when dried, becomes a useful herb. It's essential in southern French cooking, where it flavors vegetables, entrées, and desserts. In non-culinary uses, you can keep dried lavender on hand to add a clean, subtle scent to your home.*

## Ingredients
1 bunch lavender

**1.** Wash lavender and pat dry.

**2.** Spread in a single even layer across one or more dehydrator shelves. Dry at 125°F until lavender leaves crumble easily when rubbed between fingertips, about 1–2 hours.

**3.** Transfer lavender to a clean work surface and cool to room temperature, about 2 hours. Using clean, dry hands, remove leaves from stems. Transfer leaves to an airtight container and store.

## Uses

- Dried lavender is a wonderful laundry freshener. To make a sachet, sew dried lavender into muslin pouches and store in drawers with lingerie, hosiery, linens, or sweaters.
- Lavender is what gives *herbes de Provence* (a French herb blend) its characteristic scent and flavor. Make your own by combining equal parts of dried lavender, dried thyme, dried savory, dried basil, and dried marjoram or dried oregano. Use to flavor grilled vegetables, chicken, or fish.
- Creamy desserts bring out the best in lavender. It's a terrific substitution for vanilla extract when you make your favorite custard, rice pudding, or ice cream recipe.

# Bleu Cheese

*It seems counterintuitive to want to dry cheese considering the lengths cooks will go to keep cheese fresh. However, dried cheese—especially a full-flavored bleu cheese—can be a powerhouse in the kitchen, letting you add complex flavor to any dish with just a sprinkling.*

### Ingredients
½ pound firm bleu cheese, such as Roquefort or gorgonzola piccante
1 roll unbleached paper towels

..........................................................................................................

**1.** Line each dehydrator rack with a sheet of paper towel. Crumble cheese into very small pieces and transfer to prepared dehydrator racks. Spread cheese in a single, even layer.

**2.** Dehydrate cheese at 115°F. Once per hour, remove racks from dehydrator, transfer cheese to a plate, and discard oil-soaked paper towels. Re-line racks with fresh paper towels, transfer cheese to the prepared racks, and replace racks to dehydrator.

**3.** Continue to dehydrate the cheese until it is very firm to the touch, 10–12 hours. Transfer cheese to a baking sheet in a single, even layer. Allow to cool to room temperature, about 1 hour.

**4.** Transfer cheese to an airtight container and store at room temperature up to 1 week.

..........................................................................................................

### Freshen the Towels

When dehydrating cheese, the milk fat in the cheese separates from the milk solids. Paper towels can absorb this milk fat. Changing the towels hourly ensures that the milk fat remains separate from the cheese solids, and also prevents the cheese from sticking to the paper towels.

..........................................................................................................

### Uses

- Mix dried bleu cheese with candied pecans or walnuts and dried cranberries to make an adult trail mix that is also perfect to serve at any cocktail party.
- Make a compound butter for steaks. Soften a stick of unsalted butter. Stir in ¼ cup dehydrated bleu cheese and 1 tablespoon dried chives. Roll into a tube shape in plastic wrap and chill. To serve, cut a slice of butter and place atop a cooked steak right before you eat it.
- Using a spice grinder or food processor, pulverize cheese into a fine powder. Sprinkle on snack foods such as fresh-popped popcorn. Stir into sour cream to make a bleu cheese dip for crudités. Or, rim a martini glass with bleu cheese powder when you're serving vodka or gin martinis that are garnished with bleu cheese-stuffed olives.

# Cheddar Cheese

*Rather than freeze leftover Cheddar, dehydrate it. The drying process intensifies its flavor, letting you add an instant cheesy kick to your dishes. This recipe works well for white or yellow Cheddar. Aged Cheddar will dry more quickly because it has less moisture than younger Cheddars, so be sure to monitor the cheese-drying process carefully.*

## Ingredients

1 pound sharp Cheddar cheese, finely grated
1 roll unbleached paper towels

......................................................................................................

**1.** Line two or more dehydrator racks with paper towels. Sprinkle cheese onto prepared dehydrator racks, ensuring cheese is in a single, even layer.

**2.** Dehydrate cheese at 115°F. Once per hour, remove racks from dehydrator, transfer cheese to a plate, and discard oil-soaked paper towels. Re-line racks with fresh paper towels, transfer cheese to the prepared racks, and replace racks in dehydrator.

**3.** Continue to dehydrate the cheese until it is very firm to the touch, 10–12 hours. Transfer cheese to a baking sheet in a single, even layer. Allow to cool to room temperature, about 1 hour.

**4.** Transfer cheese to an airtight container and store at room temperature up to 1 week.

## Uses

- Rehydrate dried Cheddar in simmering milk to make a quick cheese sauce or soup. Add ¼ cup dried Cheddar to each cup of milk. For a thicker consistency, add 1 tablespoon cold water that has been mixed with 1 tablespoon cornstarch. Serve over cooked green vegetables.
- Make Cheddar cheese powder by pulverizing in a spice grinder or small food processor. Substitute one for one with commercial cheese powder.

......................................................................................................

### Kick Up Your Bread

If you love making your own breads, one tasty addition is a few tablespoons of dried cheese powder. Or take it one step further and add some dried onion, chives, or even sun-dried tomatoes for a gourmet treat that's half the cost of store-bought.

......................................................................................................

# Parmesan Cheese

*Like mushrooms and tomatoes, Parmesan cheese packs a hefty dose of the flavor umami. And, like the other two ingredients, it can be helpful when cooking vegetable dishes for meat lovers. Dehydrating Parmesan cheese will intensify its flavor and substantially lengthen its shelf life.*

## Ingredients

1 pound aged Parmesan cheese, finely grated
1 roll unbleached paper towels

**1.** Line two or more dehydrator racks with paper towels. Sprinkle cheese onto prepared dehydrator racks, ensuring cheese is in a single, even layer.

**2.** Dehydrate cheese at 115°F. Once per hour, remove racks from dehydrator, transfer cheese to a plate, and discard oil-soaked paper towels. Re-line racks with fresh paper towels, transfer cheese to the prepared racks, and replace racks in dehydrator.

**3.** Continue to dehydrate the cheese until it is very firm to the touch, 10–12 hours. Transfer cheese to a baking sheet in a single, even layer. Allow to cool to room temperature, about 1 hour.

**4.** Transfer cheese to an airtight container and store at room temperature up to 1 week.

## Uses

- Instantly upgrade your salad dressing to an Italian delight. Stir dried Parmesan into ranch dressing, vinaigrette, or even creamy garlic dressing.
- When baking French bread, rolls, or crescent rolls, top dough with dried Parmesan and a mixture of dried Italian herbs—like basil and oregano—brush with oil and bake as usual. Or for store-bought bread, make a quick garlic butter. Crush a clove of garlic and mince finely. Add ½ stick softened unsalted butter, and 1 tablespoon dried Parmesan.
- For a finer consistency, pulverize cheese into a fine powder using a spice grinder or food processor.

# Tofu

*Packed with protein, iron, and calcium, yet low in calories, tofu is a great addition to many diets. However, tofu spoils quickly, and requires several changes of water during storage in order to stay fresh. To reduce the hassle of keeping tofu, you can dehydrate it. Dried tofu is a staple in Japan, where it is used after rehydrating. It's recommended that you use extra-firm tofu for dehydrating, because it will take the least amount of time. However, if you have firm or silken tofu, you can dry those. The process will simply take longer.*

## Ingredients
1 pound extra-firm tofu
1 roll unbleached paper towels

...................................................................................................................................

**1.** Remove tofu from packaging, discarding liquid. Cut into ¼" slices.
**2.** Dry tofu: Place two pieces paper towel onto a clean work surface. Place a single even layer of tofu onto paper towel and cover with two additional pieces of paper towel. Press gently to remove excess liquid from tofu. Remove top layers of paper towel and discard. Remove tofu and set aside. Discard two bottom paper towels. Repeat process with remaining tofu.
**3.** Cut tofu slices into ¼" cubes.
**4.** Spread tofu cubes in a single even layer across one or more dehydrator shelves. Dry at 125°F until tofu shrinks by half and is slightly chewy, about 2–3 hours.
**5.** Transfer tofu to a clean work surface and cool to room temperature, about 2 hours. Transfer to an airtight container and store.

## Uses
- Rehydrate dried tofu, drain, pat dry, and sauté it in peanut oil. Add your favorite vegetables and stir-fry to make a side dish or a protein-packed main meal.
- Make a snack mix for your next Asian-inspired dinner party. Mix dried tofu with soy-glazed rice crackers and wasabi peas. Delicious with sake cocktails!
- Add dried tofu to a smoothie for a quick addition of protein. Because dried tofu has a neutral flavor, it will not materially affect the taste of your smoothie, and you can add it to your favorite recipe. As tofu is high in iron, you may want to add ingredients with a high amount of vitamin C, such as berries or citrus fruit, to help your body use the iron in tofu.

# Yogurt

*Homemade yogurt is so much tastier than store-bought yogurt that you may never buy yogurt again. A dehydrator can serve the same purpose as a yogurt maker, by holding the yogurt at 115°F until it thickens. For this recipe, you will need a thermometer to ensure that your initial mixture cools to the correct temperature before transferring it to your dehydrator.*

## Ingredients
1 quart milk (whole, skim, or 2%)
8 ounces plain yogurt, matched to the fat content of the milk (for example, if you are making whole milk, use a whole-milk yogurt)

......................................................................................................................................

**1.** Place milk in a large pot and bring to a boil over medium heat. Boil 1 minute.
**2.** Remove from heat and cool milk at room temperature until it reaches 110°F, about 10 minutes.
**3.** Place yogurt in a medium bowl. Add ½ cup of milk and whisk until completely combined. Repeat process, incorporating milk into yogurt by ½ cups, until you have added all milk.
**4.** Pour mixture through a wire mesh strainer into 6- to 8-ounce ramekins.
**5.** Place ramekins onto one or more dehydrator shelves. Dehydrate at 115°F until yogurt is thick and creamy, about 8–10 hours.
**6.** Remove ramekins from dehydrator and allow to cool on a wire rack to room temperature, about an hour. Cover and refrigerate.

## Uses
- Top with dried fruits, nuts, and granola to create a quick dessert.
- Use yogurt in place of sour cream in your favorite recipes.
- Blend with your favorite fruits and freeze into pops to make a healthy cool treat for summer.

# Sriracha

*Sriracha is a hot sauce native to Thailand. It's made from red-hot Thai chili peppers, sugar, spices, and vinegar. You will find sriracha, along with Thai chili paste (nam prik pao), in most Thai restaurants. Just a little sauce adds a good dose of heat and a slight sourness to dishes. Dehydrating sriracha is a great way to have the flavor of hot sauce without the moisture and is good to use as a coating or in drier dishes.*

**Ingredients**

½ cup sriracha

..................................................................................................................

**1.** Line a dehydrator shelf with aluminum foil, wax paper, or plastic wrap.

**2.** Spread sriracha in a thin, even layer over prepared dehydrator shelf. Dehydrate at 145°F until completely dried and crushes easily between fingertips, about 3–4 hours.

**3.** Transfer sriracha to a clean work surface and cool to room temperature, about 2 hours. Transfer to an airtight container and store.

**Uses**

- Sprinkle dried sriracha over a Thai barbecue chicken pizza instead of the crushed red chili that you would normally use to top pizza.
- Stir into orange marmalade and brush on roast pork for a quick Thai-style main dish.
- Make an alternative hot chili powder by pulverizing in a spice grinder or small food processor. Sriracha will have a slight tang that results from the vinegar in the sauce. Substitute one for one with commercial chili powder.

# PART III

# Prepare Delectable Recipes Using Your Dried Food

We've saved the best for last. In this final section we'll show

you how to put your dehydrated fruits, vegetables, meat, and

seafood to good use. You'll find recipes ranging from a sim-

ple but flavor-packed lemonade to lamb stew and beef bris-

ket, and let's not forget an array of mouth-watering desserts.

So roll up your sleeves, sort through those dried goodies, and

let's get cooking.

# CHAPTER 8
# Amuse-Bouche

Amuse-bouche is a French phrase that translates into "delighted mouth" or "tasty bite." The amuse-bouche course in a restaurant is often a single-bite appetizer that gets the diner ready for the meal, and is frequently made with ingredients the restaurant already has on hand. You can mimic this tradition at home by creating your own starters with ingredients you have on hand. And by relying on dehydrated ingredients, these amuse-bouche recipes come together in a snap.

# Arancini

**Makes 16 bite-sized arancini, or the perfect appetizer for 8.**

*This is a delicious appetizer with which to begin an Italian feast. It's perfect with leftover risotto. When making Dried Mushroom Risotto (see Chapter 11), make a batch and a half so that you have leftovers to make arancini. Try serving them with warmed marinara sauce for dipping.*

## Ingredients

1 cup chilled Dried Mushroom Risotto, or your favorite risotto recipe

½ cup flour

½ teaspoon salt, divided

1 egg

½ cup bread crumbs or panko-style breadcrumbs

½ teaspoon dried basil, rosemary, sage, or oregano

4 or more cups vegetable oil

**1.** Line a baking sheet with waxed paper. Measure a tablespoon of chilled risotto and roll into a ball. Place on prepared baking sheet. Repeat with remaining risotto.

**2.** Place flour into a small, deep bowl and season with half the salt. Break egg into a second small, deep bowl. Beat with remaining salt. Place breadcrumbs and dried herbs into a third small, deep bowl.

**3.** Dredge each rice ball in flour and return to baking sheet. When finished, roll each rice ball in beaten egg and return to baking sheet. Finally, roll each rice ball in breadcrumbs and return to baking sheet.

**4.** Line a second baking sheet with paper towels, or place a wire rack onto baking sheet.

**5.** Heat 4 cups of oil in a heavy skillet until hot, but not smoking. If you have a candy thermometer, the oil should reach 350°F.

**6.** Add 4 rice balls to oil and fry until golden brown, about 5–6 minutes, turning occasionally to ensure all surfaces come in contact with the oil. Remove fried rice balls from oil with a slotted spoon, placing onto the baking sheet with paper towel or the rack. If rice balls have absorbed too much of the frying oil, add more oil to the skillet and heat to 350°F.

**7.** Repeat with remaining rice balls. Serve immediately.

### One Dish . . . But Lots of Choices

This is another dish that's perfect for giving your own culinary spin. Just about any type of risotto can be used, and all you need to do is vary the seasoning in the coating. Try black beans and sweet potatoes in the risotto with a spicy coating of chili powder and cumin or even chipotle chili pepper.

Dehydrated Carrots

Goat Cheese Rolled in Beet Powder

House-Made Bleu Cheese Potato Chips

Palmiers with Spinach-Cheese Filling

Strawberry-Basil Lemonade

Sriracha-Dusted Chicken Skewers with Creamy Peanut Sauce

Red Lentil Soup with Dried Carrot and Cumin Tadka

Thai Curried Butternut Squash Soup with
Toasted Coconut and Dried Pears

Curried Chicken Salad with Dried Coconut
and Dried Pineapple

Pico de Gallo Quinoa Salad

Sweet and Sour Kale Salad
with Dried Cherries

White Bean and Haricots Verts Salad with Dried Chive and Dried Lemon Vinaigrette

Beef with Dried Brandied Cherries

Spice and Chili–Rubbed Pulled Pork

Grilled Tuna with Papaya Relish

Edamame Sauté with Dried Tofu,
Mushrooms, and Ginger

Roasted Carrots and Parsnips with
Dried Autumn Fruits

Baked Falafel with Tahini-Mint Dressing

Chocolate-Dipped Fruits

Cranberry Sauce Bars with
Dried Mixed Berries

Sautéed Brussels Sprouts with Raisins,
White Wine, and Dijon Mustard

Spiced Chili Pepper Hot Chocolate

Untraditional Trifle

Vanilla Bean Gelato with Dried Strawberries

# Balsamic and Herb Cocktail Nuts

**Makes 8 servings.**

*Cocktail nuts are so named because they are perfect for having with cocktails—effortless to eat, slightly salty, and a good match to spirits.*

## Ingredients

1 pound raw almonds

1 tablespoon butter, melted

1 tablespoon balsamic vinegar

2 teaspoons dried herbs (rosemary, basil, thyme, sage, or a combination)

½ teaspoon cayenne

2 teaspoons brown sugar

2 teaspoons salt

**1.** Preheat oven to 375°F.

**2.** Spread almonds in a single even layer on a baking sheet and bake, checking every 3–4 minutes and stirring, until they are lightly toasted and warmed through, about 10 minutes.

**3.** Meanwhile, combine butter, balsamic vinegar, herbs, cayenne, brown sugar, and salt in a large bowl. Add almonds and toss until nuts are completely coated. Serve warm.

### A Super Bowl Staple

You'll be a hit at the next party when you serve these. They're great for holiday entertaining and for nibbling during football games. Like most recipes, nothing's set in stone so try mixing and matching different herbs and spices. Try cashews with curry, pecans with Cajun spices, or even peanuts with taco seasoning. And how about using some dried ranch dressing?

# Black Bean and Corn Chips with Salsa

**Makes 4 servings.**

*These homemade chips, made from your own dried corn, are a little sweeter and more rustic than store-bought chips. You can serve them with the salsa in this recipe or pair them with your favorite homemade or prepared salsa. You may want to avoid fruit salsas, however, as the corn in these homemade chips tastes sweet enough on its own.*

## Ingredients

2 cups dried corn

½ cup cooked black beans, rinsed and drained

Pan spray

1 cup water

2 tablespoons butter

1½ teaspoons salt, divided three ways

½ cup cornstarch, plus more for dusting

½ teaspoon dried chili powder

½ teaspoon dried garlic powder

1 large beefsteak tomato, cored and chopped into ½" pieces

¼ cup diced onion

2 tablespoons chopped cilantro

1 tablespoon minced jalapeño peppers (optional)

Juice of ½ lime

1. Preheat oven to 375°F.
2. In a spice grinder or food processor, pulverize dried corn into a fine powder. Transfer to a large bowl.
3. Place black beans in a bowl and coarsely mash with a potato masher. Beans should be partially chunky and partially smooth.
4. Spray two baking sheets with pan spray, or lightly oil two baking sheets.
5. Bring water, butter, and ½ teaspoon salt to a boil. Pour mixture over corn meal and stir well. Mix in mashed beans. Let dough rest until cooled, about 20 minutes.
6. Mix in cornstarch by tablespoons until mixture is as firm as pie dough.
7. Dust a clean, dry work surface with cornstarch. Divide dough into four even pieces. Roll each piece into a ball and transfer to work surface. Roll each ball into a flat disk, about the thickness of a sheet of paper. Cut each disk into 6–8 triangles. Transfer triangles to baking sheet. Repeat with remaining balls.
8. Spray chips with pan spray. Mix ½ teaspoon salt with chili powder and garlic powder. Sprinkle evenly over chips.
9. Bake chips until golden brown and crispy, about 12–14 minutes. Check halfway through baking to ensure all chips are baking evenly. Turn chips and rotate pans, if necessary.
10. Transfer to wire rack and cool to room temperature, about 30 minutes.
11. While chips cool, make salsa. Mix together tomatoes, onion, cilantro, (jalapeños optional), and lime juice. Season to taste with remaining ½ teaspoon salt and pepper.
12. Once chips have cooled, serve with salsa.

# Cod Fritters with Tartar Sauce

**Makes 24 fritters, or 8 servings.**

*One of the staple foods of coastal Europe is cod, which Europeans often dehydrate into dried salt cod to sustain them during the off season. As you can imagine, salt cod is not for those who like mild flavors. However, when combined with potatoes and fried, it becomes a delicious start to any meal.*

## Ingredients

1 cup mayonnaise
1 teaspoon dried shallot or onion
1 teaspoon dried dill
¼ cup sweet pickle relish
1 tablespoon fresh lemon juice
½ pound dried salt cod or dried salmon
1 pound baking potatoes (such as russet), peeled and cut into 1" pieces
1 teaspoon dried garlic powder
2 tablespoons unsalted butter
½ onion, peeled and cut into ¼" dice
3 large eggs
1½ cups or more flour
1½ cups or more panko-style breadcrumbs
4 cups vegetable oil

**1.** Make tartar sauce: Place mayonnaise, shallots or onion, dill, relish, and lemon juice into a small bowl and mix. Cover and refrigerate until ready to use.

**2.** Place salt cod into a large non-reactive baking dish and cover by 1" with cold water. Soak 2–3 days, keeping in refrigerator. Drain and replace water 3–4 times per day.

**3.** Drain cod and transfer to a large pot. Cover with fresh water. Add potatoes and garlic powder. Bring to a boil and cook until fish flakes easily and potatoes are cooked, about 20 minutes. Drain completely and transfer mixture to a single layer on a baking sheet. Let rest until excess moisture is evaporated, about 20 minutes.

**4.** Transfer mixture to a large bowl and mash into a coarse paste with a potato masher.

**5.** Melt butter in a large pan over medium-low heat. When melted, add onion and cook, stirring frequently, until onion is limp and translucent, about 8 minutes. Add to bowl with cod and potatoes, scraping liquid into bowl. Taste mixture and add salt, if necessary. Add 1 egg and mix thoroughly. Transfer to refrigerator until completely chilled and firm, about 1 hour.

**6.** Remove mixture from refrigerator and form into 24 ball-shaped fritters, 1" in diameter. If fritters do not hold together, add flour by tablespoons until mixture is stiff enough to hold its shape.

**7.** Roll each fritter in flour, shaking to remove excess.

# Cod Fritters with Tartar Sauce
## (continued)

**8.** Beat remaining eggs together. Roll each fritter into egg mixture, allowing excess egg to drip off.

**9.** Roll each fritter into panko breadcrumbs and set onto a wire rack. Transfer to refrigerator and chill 20 minutes.

**10.** Heat oil in a large, heavy skillet over medium-high heat. When oil is hot but not smoking, add 6 fritters and cook, turning occasionally, until golden brown on all sides, about 5 minutes. Transfer fritters to a baking sheet lined with paper towels. Repeat with remaining fritters, cooking in batches of 6 at a time.

**11.** Serve warm with tartar sauce.

# Dried Guava and Cream Cheese Finger Sandwiches with Lime Curd

**Makes 4 servings.**

*You don't need to host a high tea in order to serve finger sandwiches. These tropical delights are fun and easy to eat, and are right at home either as a starting course, on a buffet, or as a light lunch with a salad. If you don't have dried guava on hand, substitute any dried tropical fruit, such as dried mango or dried pineapple. For an extra treat, butter edges of the cut sandwiches and roll in dried coconut.*

## Ingredients
8 slices whole-wheat bread
4 tablespoons cream cheese, softened
2 tablespoons lime curd (may substitute lemon curd)
2 tablespoons dried guava, diced

**1.** Place 4 slices of bread on a clean work surface. Spread one side of each slice with 1 tablespoon cream cheese.
**2.** Top each slice with ½ tablespoon of lime (or lemon) curd. Sprinkle each slice with ½ tablespoon dried guava. Top each slice with a second slice of bread.
**3.** Trim crusts from each sandwich. Cut each sandwich into thirds, lengthwise. Serve.

# Goat Cheese Rolled in Beet Powder

**Makes 4 servings.**

*Beet powder is a sweet, yet earthy ingredient. The flavor pairs exceptionally well with tangy goat cheese. For the holidays, try rolling part of the goat cheese in beet powder and part of the goat cheese in dried parsley to make a festive green and red pattern.*

## Ingredients
½ cup dehydrated beets
1 (4-ounce) roll fresh goat cheese
Assorted crackers

**1.** Using a food processor, blender, or spice grinder, process dehydrated beets into a fine powder. Transfer to a shallow bowl.

**2.** Roll goat cheese in beet powder to cover. Serve with crackers.

### Made to Impress

Sometimes just two ingredients can produce a crowd-pleasing recipe. In this case a root vegetable and gourmet cheese burst together on your palate for a rich and sweet combo. Beet powder's deep red hues are perfect for any holiday platter. Try pairing it with other cheeses and fruits. Your guests will be smiling and you will too because you know how easy it was to make.

# Grilled Shrimp Skewers with Dried Mango Chutney

**Makes 8 servings.**

*Plump grilled shrimp meets its match with an aromatic chutney based on dried mango. Unlike your typical chutneys, in which the fruit has to cook down, you can make this chutney as quickly as you preheat your grill and cook the shrimp because it relies on dried mango. It's also delicious with other dried fruits, such as fig, peach, or nectarine. And if you're not in the mood for shrimp, the chutney tastes terrific on chicken, pork, or fish, or alongside cheese on a cheese tray.*

## Ingredients

1 cup dried mango, chopped into ½" pieces

¼ cup dried bell peppers

¼ cup dried scallions or onions

¼ cup raisins

2 tablespoons brown sugar

½ teaspoon dried ground garlic

½ teaspoon dried ground ginger

1 small cinnamon stick

¼ teaspoon whole cloves

1 pinch cayenne pepper

1 tablespoon cider or white distilled vinegar

½ teaspoon salt

¼ teaspoon pepper

1 pound raw large shrimp, peeled and deveined

16–20 wooden skewers, soaked in water 30 minutes

**1.** Make the chutney. Rinse dried mango, peppers, onions, and raisins together in a wire mesh sieve. Place in a small, heavy saucepan and just barely cover with water. Bring to a boil, then turn down heat. Simmer, uncovered, until fruit is soft, about 8–10 minutes.

**2.** Add sugar, garlic, ginger, cinnamon, cloves, and cayenne. Increase heat to medium and cook, stirring frequently, until thick, about 10 minutes.

**3.** Transfer to bowl. Remove cinnamon stick and cloves using tongs or a spoon (careful—mixture will be hot). Mix in vinegar, and season to taste with salt and pepper. Chill to room temperature, about 30 minutes.

**4.** Preheat grill to medium.

**5.** Thread one shrimp per skewer. Season on both sides with salt and pepper.

**6.** Grill shrimp until pink on one side, about 3 minutes. Turn and cook until just pink on the second side, about 2 minutes.

**7.** Transfer shrimp to a clean platter and serve with chutney.

# House-Made Bleu Cheese Potato Chips

**Makes 8 servings.**

*Making your own potato chips may seem like a daunting task, but they are fairly simple if you get two things right: slicing the potatoes wafer thin, and ensuring the oil is hot enough before you begin frying the chips. One trick is to heat the oil while you slice potatoes. Although a mandoline is ideal for making this recipe, you can hand-slice the potatoes.*

## Ingredients

4 firm baking potatoes, such as russet or Yukon gold

8 cups or more vegetable oil

Clean paper bag

1 recipe bleu cheese powder

Pan spray

**1.** Scrub potatoes clean. Peel, if desired. Slice into paper-thin slices using a mandoline, food processor, or sharp knife. Toss potatoes in a large bowl with a few tablespoons of oil to prevent browning.

**2.** Place remaining oil in a large, heavy saucepot. Heat over medium-high heat, until oil is 375°F. (If you don't have a high-heat thermometer, one indication that the oil is hot enough is to add one drop of water to the oil. It should immediately sizzle.)

**3.** Working in batches, fry potatoes until they are golden brown, about 3–5 minutes per batch. If the level of oil lowers more than an inch, add oil and bring back to 375°F before adding more potatoes. Transfer potatoes to a metal colander or metal rack to drain.

**4.** Once you've cooked all potatoes, transfer to a paper bag with cheese powder. Shake to coat potatoes. If you find the cheese doesn't stick, remove chips from bag and spray with pan spray. Return to bag and shake again. Serve.

### One Potato, Two Potato

It's not just white potatoes that make a great snack like this one. Try using sweet potatoes and then adding spices like cumin or even curry powder. Serve them at your next party and guests will ask you where you bought them.

# Manchego and Quince Paste

**Makes 8 servings.**

*Quince paste, also known as membrillo, originated in Spain, and came to Latin America with the Spaniards. In the Americas and Caribbean, membrillo was adapted and made with local fruit, such as guava or papaya, and can refer to any thick fruit paste. Whether made with quince or tropical fruit, it's an ideal companion for cheese. In Spain, the quintessential pairing is quince membrillo with manchego, a ripened sheep's milk cheese made in the La Mancha region of Spain.*

## Ingredients
1 serving Quince Paste (see recipe in Chapter 5)
1 pound manchego cheese
Assorted crackers

. . . . . . . . . . . . . . . . . . . . . . . . . . . . . . . . . . . . . . . . . . . . . . . . . . . . . . . . . . . . . . . . . . . . . . . . . . . . . . . . . . . . . . . . . . . . . . . . . . . . . . . . . . . . . . . . . .

**1.** Cut manchego cheese into triangles that are roughly the same size as the quince paste triangles. Place a piece of manchego onto a cracker, top with quince paste, and serve.

# Mushroom Deviled Eggs

**Makes 6 appetizer servings.**

*Mushrooms add a savory flavor to any dish, and naturally enhance the taste of eggs. Once you have dehydrated mushrooms on hand, it's a breeze to powder them and add them to deviled eggs. You could also make this recipe with dehydrated tomato powder instead of mushroom.*

## Ingredients
6 large eggs
5–6 slices dried mushrooms or 2–3 small mushroom caps
2 tablespoons mayonnaise
¼ teaspoon or more salt

**1.** Place eggs in a large saucepot and cover with 1"–2" cold water. Place over high heat and bring to a rolling boil. Turn off heat and cover pot. Leave eggs in hot water for 15 minutes. Drain and place eggs in ice water for 5 minutes.

**2.** As eggs are cooling, place dried mushrooms into a mini food processor or spice grinder. Pulse-grind until completely powdered, about 30 pulses.

**3.** Peel eggs and halve lengthwise. Carefully remove yolks and mash in a bowl with a fork. Add mayonnaise, mushroom powder, and salt and combine completely. Transfer yolk mixture to a 1-quart zipper storage bag, cut the corner off the bag, and pipe mixture evenly into the egg white halves. Garnish with additional mushroom powder, if desired.

### Egg Salad Sandwiches
While these make wonderful snacks and party fare, they make a great sandwich filling too. Mix the egg yolks and whites together, and add the rest of the ingredients and blend. Presto, gourmet egg salad that's perfect for sandwiches, pitas, and even stuffed tomatoes on a hot summer's day.

# Onion Dip

**Makes 2 cups, enough for 8–10 servings.**

*It's simple to buy ready-made onion dip (or even a spice packet for onion dip) in the store, but once you make onion dip from your own dehydrated vegetables, you're unlikely to take that route. Rich and full of flavor, this dip is easy to make any time you have dried onions. It's especially delicious when you mix different types of onions.*

## Ingredients

½ cup dried mixed onions, green onions, and shallots

¾ cup sour cream

¾ cup mayonnaise

½ teaspoon dried garlic powder

½ teaspoon dry mustard powder

1 teaspoon Worcestershire sauce

¼ teaspoon ground black pepper

½ teaspoon salt

1–2 tablespoons milk, optional

Cut raw vegetables and/or potato chips for dipping

**1.** Place all ingredients except milk into a medium bowl and stir gently to combine. For a thinner consistency, add optional milk by teaspoons until you reach the desired consistency.

**2.** Cover and chill until flavors are melded and onions have softened, about 45 minutes. Serve with vegetables or potato chips.

### Maximize Freshness

You can make this dip up to 1 week in advance. To ensure optimal freshness, cover tightly and keep toward the back of your refrigerator.

# Palmiers with Spinach-Cheese Filling

**Makes 16–20 pieces, or 8 servings.**

*These savory pastries, named palmiers because of their resemblance to palm leaves, are the perfect use for dried vegetables. You would typically make palmiers with fresh or frozen spinach, which is labor-intensive to cook and wring dry. This recipe calls for dried spinach instead, which is not only quick to turn into a filling, but also has a more intense flavor than fresh spinach. Make a double batch and freeze one before baking. That way, you can simply slice and bake palmiers any time you'd like a savory snack.*

## Ingredients

½ cup cream cheese, softened

½ cup crumbled feta cheese

1 cup dried spinach leaves

1 teaspoon garlic powder

1 tablespoon olive oil

1 teaspoon dried dill

1 sheet frozen puff pastry dough, thawed according to package directions

**1.** Place cream cheese, feta, spinach, garlic powder, oil, and dill into a medium bowl. Stir well to combine.

**2.** Place dough onto a work surface and unfold into a single layer. Roll into an 8" × 10" rectangle. Spread spinach-cheese mixture onto dough in an even layer, leaving a ½" border on the two long sides.

**3.** Roll each of the two long sides of the dough toward the middle so that the dough meets in the middle and looks like a scroll. Transfer to a baking sheet and chill until firm, about 20–30 minutes.

**4.** Preheat oven to 400°F.

**5.** Remove roll from refrigerator and transfer to a cutting board. Cut crosswise into roughly 16–20 thin slices. Place slices onto baking sheets, leaving ½" of space between them. Bake until crispy and golden brown, about 15–20 minutes. Transfer to a wire rack, allow to cool 3 minutes, and serve.

# Sriracha-Dusted Chicken Skewers with Creamy Peanut Sauce

**Makes 8 appetizer servings or 4 entrée servings.**

*This riff on chicken satay pairs traditional Thai peanut dipping sauce with the fiery heat of dried sriracha. If you don't have dehydrated sriracha, feel free to substitute another homemade dried chili powder mixed with salt.*

## Ingredients

¼ cup dried sriracha powder (may substitute ¼ cup dried chili pepper powder mixed with ½ teaspoon salt)

1 pound boneless, skinless chicken breasts, cut into 1" pieces

16 wooden skewers, soaked in water 30 minutes

¾ cup cocktail peanuts

1 tablespoon peanut oil or vegetable oil (preferably peanut)

½ teaspoon dried garlic

½ teaspoon dried ginger

¼–½ cup water

¼ cup soy sauce or tamari

¼ cup fresh lime juice

¼ cup honey

¼ cup cilantro, chopped (optional)

1. Preheat indoor or outdoor grill to medium heat.
2. Sprinkle sriracha powder over chicken pieces in an even layer. Thread 1–2 chicken pieces onto each skewer.
3. Make dipping sauce: Place peanuts, oil, garlic, ginger, water, tamari, lime juice, and honey into the bowl of a food processor or blender. Purée, stopping occasionally to scrape bowl, until mixture is smooth. Adjust mixture to desired consistency by adding water by tablespoons.
4. Transfer sauce to a serving bowl.
5. Grill chicken skewers until brown on one side, about 4–5 minutes. Turn over and grill until the other side is brown and chicken is cooked through, about 3–4 minutes.
6. Transfer chicken to a clean platter. Serve with peanut dipping sauce and sprinkle with cilantro, if desired.

### Try Some PB

Want an extra creamy peanut sauce for this dish? Leave out the peanuts and substitute ¼ cup of peanut butter. It makes for an extra silky sauce that tastes gourmet and will have everyone thinking you spent hours making it.

# Strawberry-Basil Lemonade

**Makes 4 servings.**

*A fresh pink lemonade made with a hint of herbs is refreshing on a hot day. This recipe is equally delicious whether made with sparkling or still water, and is even tastier when you add your favorite vodka.*

## Ingredients

4 lemons

¾ cup sugar

1 cup water

2 tablespoons dried strawberries

1 teaspoon dried basil

2 cups chilled water, still or sparkling

Additional dried strawberries, to garnish

**1.** Wash lemons and remove zest with a microplane, zester, or a fine-gauge grater. Place zest into a 2-cup heatproof container.

**2.** Juice lemons, straining out seeds, and set aside.

**3.** Make flavored simple syrup: Mix together sugar and water in a small saucepan. Bring to a boil and simmer until sugar is completely dissolved, about 1 minute. Pour sugar water over lemon zest. Add strawberries and basil and steep, uncovered, 20 minutes.

**4.** Strain mixture through a wire mesh strainer and allow to cool completely, about 30 additional minutes.

**5.** Add reserved lemon juice and still or sparkling water with cool simple syrup. Serve over ice, garnished with additional dried strawberries.

### Summer Year-Round

Lemonade doesn't have to be a summer-only drink as this recipe proves. When you have dried fruits on hand you can make beverages like this even in the dead of winter. Try substituting any combination of fruit and herbs, like peach and mint or even raspberry and thyme.

# Sun-Dried Tomatoes, Fresh Ricotta & Rosemary, with Balsamic Glaze

**Makes 8 servings as an appetizer portion or 4 servings as a salad portion.**

*When you have dried tomatoes on hand, you are never that far away from a great appetizer. Rehydrated and marinated in a fragrant oil, dehydrated tomatoes make the perfect base for canapés. Here, you top them with ricotta cheese so that the natural flavors of tomato can shine through. Any soft mild cheese, such as brie or farmer's cheese, will work in this recipe.*

## Ingredients

24 sun-dried, dehydrated, or oven-dried tomatoes (each tomato piece should be at least 1" in diameter)

1 teaspoon dried rosemary

2 tablespoons extra-virgin olive oil

½ cup balsamic vinegar

4 tablespoons fresh ricotta cheese

.......................................................................................................

**1.** Rinse sun-dried tomatoes in a wire mesh strainer under cold running water. Cover with hot water until softened, about 20 minutes. Drain.

**2.** Toss tomatoes and rosemary with oil and set aside.

**3.** Meanwhile, make glaze: Bring vinegar to a boil in a small heavy saucepan. Reduce heat to medium and cook until vinegar is reduced to 2 tablespoons and is as thick as honey, about 10–15 minutes. Remove from heat and transfer to a small bowl. Cool completely.

**4.** To assemble appetizers, drain tomatoes, reserving oil with rosemary. Place ½ teaspoon ricotta atop each tomato. Drizzle with balsamic glaze and reserved oil. Serve at room temperature.

.......................................................................................................

### Gifts in the Making

If you can resist eating the sun-dried tomatoes, they make the perfect gift. Just add them to olive oil and rosemary and place in a fancy jar. Tie a ribbon around it and it's a gift for the holidays or even a thoughtful housewarming token.

.......................................................................................................

# CHAPTER 9
# Soups and Salads

Dried foods are naturally suited to use in soups. You already have simmering liquid, the basis for optimal rehydrating. What may surprise you, however, is how much dried foods will enhance a salad. In the past, you may have added raisins or dried cherries to a green salad; this section helps you expand on that repertoire, by showing you how dried vegetables and dried shellfish can enhance your next salad.

# Chicken Mushroom Soup with Soba Noodles

**Makes 8 servings.**

*This hearty soup comes together quickly and makes an ideal midweek meal. Since you use dried mushrooms and dried scallions, there is hardly any prep. If you plan to make this soup one day and serve it another, keep the cooked noodles separate from the rest of the broth. Otherwise, they begin to break down and thicken the soup.*

## Ingredients

1 pound boneless, skinless chicken breasts or chicken thighs, cut into long, narrow strips

2 tablespoons soy sauce

2 tablespoons sake or dry sherry

2 tablespoons honey

1 tablespoon sesame oil

½ cup dried mushrooms, preferably shiitake

¼ cup dried green onions

1" ginger, peeled and cut into ¼"-thick slices

8 cups chicken stock

½ pound soba (Japanese buckwheat noodles), broken in half

**1.** Place chicken, soy sauce, sake, honey, and sesame oil in a bowl. Toss to coat chicken evenly with marinade. Cover with plastic wrap and marinate in the lowest part of your refrigerator for 30 minutes–2 hours.

**2.** Rinse mushrooms and green onions under cold running water. Place ginger slices in a tea ball or a cheesecloth pouch so that you may easily remove ginger later.

**3.** Place mushrooms, green onions, and ginger in a large pot with chicken stock and bring to a boil. Reduce heat and simmer until vegetables are softened, about 20 minutes.

**4.** Cook soba according to package directions. Drain, cool, and set aside.

**5.** Remove chicken from marinade and add to simmering stock. Cook soup until chicken is cooked through, about 2 minutes. Remove ginger. Taste soup, and add salt if necessary.

**6.** Add cooked noodles to soup and cook until noodles are hot, about 1 minute. Serve soup immediately.

# Chili

**Makes 8 servings.**

*When you make chili from chili peppers you dry yourself, you won't believe the incredible taste improvement over making chili with store-bought ones. Not only are the dried peppers fresher, and therefore more potent, but you can create a proprietary blend of pepper types that suits your palate best. In addition, you'll be sure of exactly what's going into your chili.*

## Ingredients

3–4 large dried chili peppers (such as ancho, ripe jalapeño, or pasilla)

1 teaspoon salt

2 tablespoons vegetable oil

1 pound ground beef, turkey, chicken, or pork

1 onion, peeled and cut into ¼" dice

3 cloves garlic, minced

12 ounces beer

1 (28-ounce) can tomato purée

½ cup dried green peppers

1 tablespoon cumin seeds

1 tablespoon Worcestershire sauce

½ pound dried black beans, soaked, cooked until tender, and drained [may substitute 1 (16-ounce) can black beans, rinsed and drained]

---

**1.** Place dried chilies and salt into the bowl of a spice grinder or food processor. Pulverize until completely powdered.

**2.** Heat oil in a large Dutch oven over medium heat. Add meat and onions and sprinkle with chili-salt mixture. Cook, stirring constantly, until meat is no longer pink and onions are translucent, about 10 minutes. Add garlic and cook an additional 30 seconds.

**3.** Add beer and turn heat to high. Bring to a boil and cook until beer has evaporated, about 3 minutes. Immediately add tomato purée, green peppers, cumin, Worcestershire, and beans. Bring to a boil, then reduce heat. Simmer until peppers soften and flavors combine, about 1–1½ hours.

# Congee (Rice Soup) with Dried Scallops

**Makes 8 servings.**

*Congee is a thick rice soup made throughout Asia and the variations in ingredients are endless. Typically made with rice, water, and a few seasonings, it's the perfect backdrop for marinated pork or seared shellfish. Here, it's paired with dried scallops (also known as conpoys) and fresh scallions for a hearty version. If you have some dehydrated onions or shallots on hand, sprinkle them onto a bowl of this congee to give it an extra crunch.*

## Ingredients

8 medium-sized dried scallops, divided

¾ cup uncooked white rice

1 tablespoon canola oil

½ teaspoon dried ginger powder

4 cloves garlic, minced

6–8 cups water, plus more for rinsing rice

2 cups bottled clam juice

2 tablespoons soy sauce or tamari

1 teaspoon or more salt

½ teaspoon ground black pepper

½ cup chopped green onions for garnish

1. Chop dried scallops into ¼" dice. Place 2 tablespoons of chopped scallops into a bowl and cover with hot water. Set aside to use as a garnish.

2. Place rice into a large bowl and cover by an inch with tap water. Gently mix rice and water until water is cloudy. Drain rice and repeat four to six times until the water remains clear during washing (which indicates the rice is clean). Pour rice into a mesh strainer and allow to drain at least 10 minutes.

3. Heat oil in stockpot over medium heat. Add ginger and garlic and sauté until fragrant, about 30 seconds.

4. Add 6 cups water, clam juice, and soy sauce. Turn heat to high and bring to a boil. Then reduce heat to a simmer and add rice and remaining dried scallops.

5. Simmer congee over low heat until rice is completely dissolved and congee has a creamy texture, about 3–4 hours. Check once per hour, adding water if necessary.

6. Add salt and pepper to taste. Pour into bowls, top with reserved dried scallops and chopped green onions. Serve immediately.

# Corn Chowder

**Makes 8 servings.**

*Thick and rich, this chowder showcases the sweetness of both dried corn and dried bell pepper. The trick is to cut the potatoes into small pieces so that they cook in about the same time it takes to soften the vegetables. For a spicier version of the soup, substitute ¼ cup of dried hot chili peppers for the ½ cup of dried bell peppers.*

## Ingredients

2 slices bacon, cut into ¼" strips

1 large onion, diced

4–5 cups chicken or vegetable broth

1½ cups dried corn

½ cup dried red bell pepper

1 pound potatoes, scrubbed and cut into ¼"
   dice

1 teaspoon or more salt

1 cup half-and-half

½ teaspoon black pepper

Pinch cayenne pepper

. . . . . . . . . . . . . . . . . . . . . . . . . . . . . . . . . . . . . . . . . . . . . . . . . . . . . . . . . . . . . . . . . . . . . . . . . . . . . . . . . . . . . . . . . . . . . .

**1.** Heat bacon in a large pot over medium heat. Cook until oil is rendered, about 3 minutes. Add onion and cook, stirring frequently, over medium heat until onion is soft and translucent, about 6 minutes.

**2.** Add broth, corn, peppers, and potatoes. Bring to a boil, add salt, reduce heat, and simmer until corn and peppers are soft and potatoes are cooked through, about 20 minutes.

**3.** Add half-and-half and return to a simmer. Season to taste with additional salt, pepper, and cayenne.

# Fisherman's Chowder

**Makes 8 servings.**

*When you have dried scallops and shrimp on hand, you are never too far away from an indulgent seafood chowder. This recipe, which allows you to showcase your own dried shellfish as well as dried corn and herbs, also features fresh fish, making for interesting texture combinations in the bowl.*

## Ingredients

2 tablespoons unsalted butter

1 cup chopped white or yellow onion

2 pounds baking potatoes (such as russet or Yukon Gold), scrubbed, peeled, and sliced ¼" thick

5 cups bottled clam juice or vegetable stock

1 cup dried corn

½ cup dried shrimp

½ cup dried scallops

1 dried bay leaf

1 teaspoon dried thyme

½ teaspoon salt

¼ teaspoon black pepper

1 or more cups cold water

1½ pounds mild white fish (such as cod, haddock, tilapia, or trout), boneless, skinless, and cut into 1" cubes

1 cup heavy cream

2 teaspoons dried chives

**1.** Heat a large, heavy pot over low heat. Add the butter and onions and cook, stirring occasionally, until onions are translucent and soft, about 8 minutes.

**2.** Add potatoes, clam juice, corn, shrimp, scallops, bay leaf, thyme, salt, and pepper. Add water until liquid barely covers the mixture. Bring to a boil over high heat, then reduce heat to medium-low. Cover pot and cook until shrimp and scallops are soft and potatoes are cooked through, about 15 minutes.

**3.** Taste mixture and season with additional salt and pepper, if necessary.

**4.** Add fish and cook until fish is opaque, about 5 minutes. Remove from heat and stir in cream. Serve garnished with dried chives.

# Minestrone

**Makes 8 servings.**

*When you have a large assortment of different dried vegetables in your pantry, minestrone pulls them all together into one delicious and satisfying dish. One key to this soup is Parmesan broth, which you make by simmering dried Parmesan (or the ends of a wedge of Parmesan) with dried bay leaves and pepper.*

## Ingredients

½ cup dried Parmesan powder or 1 rind from a wedge of Parmesan cheese

5 whole black peppercorns

2 dried bay leaves

6 cups water

2 cups mixed dried vegetables (such as carrots, green beans, peas, corn, broccoli, cabbage, tomato)

3 tablespoons olive oil

1 white or yellow onion, cut into ¼" dice

2 cloves garlic, minced

2 pinches dried chili pepper

1 russet potato, scrubbed and cut into ½" dice

2 cups tomato-based vegetable juice, such as V-8

2–3 teaspoons salt

**1.** Place dried Parmesan, peppercorns, bay leaves, and water into a large pot and bring to a boil. Simmer until water is flavored with Parmesan, about 30 minutes.

**2.** While broth simmers, soften vegetables. Place dried vegetables together into a wire mesh sieve and rinse under cold running water. Transfer to a medium bowl, cover with hot water, and let stand until softened, about 20 minutes. Drain well.

**3.** Heat 1 tablespoon oil over medium heat in a large skillet. Add onion and cook, stirring frequently, until onion is softened and translucent, about 8 minutes. Transfer onion to a large clean pot.

**4.** Return skillet to medium heat and add 1 tablespoon oil, half of garlic and half of chili pepper. Cook until fragrant, about 30 seconds. Add half of drained dried vegetables and cook until lightly browned, about 6–8 minutes. Transfer cooked vegetables to pot with onions. Repeat with remaining oil, garlic, chili pepper, and dried vegetables.

**5.** Strain Parmesan broth into pot with vegetables. Add potato and vegetable juice and bring to a boil. Reduce heat and simmer until flavors meld and potatoes are cooked, about 30 minutes. Season to taste with salt.

# Miso Soup with Tofu

**Makes 4 servings.**

*The start of a good dinner at a Japanese restaurant, miso soup is surprisingly easy to make at home when you have white miso paste and dried tofu. Many grocers carry white miso. If your regular store doesn't, head to an Asian market or natural foods store. Dried tofu is much better in miso soup than fresh tofu is, as it keeps its form and has a nice texture in the soup.*

## Ingredients

¼ cup white miso paste

4 cups water

½ cup dried tofu cubes

2 tablespoons dried scallions

Optional: ¼ cup dried wakame (a type of
   seaweed)

**1.** Mix all ingredients in a medium pot and bring to a boil. Reduce heat and simmer until tofu and scallions are softened, about 20 minutes. Serve.

# Red Lentil Soup with Dried Carrot and Cumin Tadka

**Makes 4 servings.**

*This spicy Indian soup will warm you up on the chilliest day. The flavors of carrots and leeks come through in this hearty soup, as drying intensifies the flavor of veggies. Tadka is a traditional topping for Indian soups and dals, but if you are in a hurry when making this soup, you can skip the tadka, as the soup is flavorful without it.*

## Ingredients

1 cup red lentils

¼ cup dried carrots

¼ cup dried onions, leeks, or scallions

1 teaspoon dried powdered garlic

½ teaspoon dried powdered ginger

½ teaspoon turmeric

½ teaspoon paprika

4–6 cups water

1 teaspoon salt, or more

2 tablespoons canola oil or clarified butter (ghee)

2 cloves garlic, thinly sliced

1 teaspoon cumin seeds

**1.** Rinse lentils, dried carrots, and dried onions in a wire mesh sieve. Transfer to a large, heavy pot and add dried garlic, dried ginger, turmeric, paprika, and 4 cups water. Bring to a boil, then reduce heat to medium-low and simmer, uncovered, for 35–45 minutes, until vegetables are all very soft.

**2.** Transfer half of soup to the bowl of a blender or food processor. Purée until smooth and return to pot with other half of soup.

**3.** Thin with additional water, if desired. Add salt and simmer 10 minutes. Taste for seasoning and add salt if needed.

**4.** Heat a small skillet over medium-high heat. Add oil or ghee, garlic slices, and cumin seeds and cook until garlic is golden brown, about 20 seconds. Immediately transfer contents of skillet to a small bowl.

**5.** Serve soup piping hot, drizzled with a bit more of the oil, garlic, and cumin.

# Thai Curried Butternut Squash Soup with Toasted Coconut and Dried Pears

**Makes 8 servings.**

*One of the joys of having dried ingredients on hand is that you can use them along with their fresh version in the same dish to achieve complex flavor and textures. This soup brings together coconut in two forms—coconut milk and dried, toasted coconut—and pears in two forms—roasted and dried. Using prepared Thai chili paste with your own dried ginger creates a subtle Southeast Asian heat. If you happen to have dried shrimp or dried scallops on hand, they make an excellent garnish for the soup. Or stir in homemade yogurt for a creamy garnish that tames the heat.*

## Ingredients

1 medium (1½–2 pound) butternut squash, peeled, seeded, and cut into 1" cubes

1 medium onion, chopped

2 cloves garlic, peeled

2 pears, peeled, cored, and cut into slices

2 tablespoons extra-virgin olive oil

1 tablespoon salt

4 cups chicken or vegetable stock

1 (14-ounce) can light coconut milk

2–3 tablespoons Thai chili paste

1 teaspoon dried ginger powder

½ cup dried coconut, toasted

½ cup dried pears, cut into ¼" cubes

1. Preheat oven to 350°F.
2. In a large bowl, toss together squash, onions, garlic, pears, oil, and salt until vegetables are coated with oil and salt. Transfer in a single layer to one or more baking sheets. Wrap tightly with foil. Bake until vegetables are very tender, about 50–60 minutes. Remove foil and roast until vegetables are browned, an additional 10 minutes.
3. Scrape half of vegetables, along with their cooking juices, into the bowl of a food processor or blender. Add half of the stock, half of coconut milk, 1 tablespoon chili paste, and ginger powder and purée until smooth. Transfer to a large, heavy pot. Repeat with remaining vegetables, stock, coconut milk, and 1 tablespoon chili paste. Transfer second batch to pot with first batch.
4. Stir in toasted coconut and dried pears. Bring soup to a simmer over medium heat. Add salt and pepper to taste. If desired, stir in additional chili paste. Serve immediately.

### Easy Preparation

An easy way to peel and slice hard squashes like the butternut variety is to pierce their skin with the tine of a fork several times and then put them into the microwave for about 30 seconds to a minute, depending on their size. Be careful because they will be hot when they come out, but preparing them this way is quick and easy, and your fingers will thank you.

# Curried Chicken Salad with Dried Coconut and Dried Pineapple

**Makes 8 servings.**

*A creamy curry dressing sets the backdrop for a chicken salad that features sweet dried pineapple and toasted dried coconut. This salad comes together even more quickly if you buy pre-chopped veggies at your grocer's salad bar. For the meat, grab a rotisserie chicken. Or visit your deli counter and ask for a 1"-thick cut of roast turkey and cut it into cubes.*

## Ingredients

½ cup dried coconut

½ cup mayonnaise

½ cup plain Greek yogurt

2 tablespoons yellow curry powder

½ teaspoon salt

2 tablespoons fresh lemon juice

1½ pounds cooked chicken or turkey, cut into 1" cubes

½ cup dried pineapple

½ cup celery, diced

½ cup red onion, diced

1 cup red grapes, halved and seeded

**1.** Heat a large stainless steel or cast iron skillet over medium heat. Add dried coconut and toast, stirring constantly, until coconut is golden brown, about 7 minutes. Immediately transfer coconut to a plate to cool.

**2.** In a large bowl, mix together mayonnaise, yogurt, curry powder, salt, and lemon juice. If necessary, add salt to taste.

**3.** Mix in chicken, pineapple, celery, onion, and red grapes. Sprinkle salad with toasted coconut and serve.

## Make Your Own

Don't worry if you don't have any Greek yogurt to make this dish because making your own is easy. All you need is some plain yogurt, some cheesecloth, a strainer, and a bowl. Line the strainer with cheesecloth and put it over a large bowl. Pour the yogurt into the strainer and place in the fridge for about 6 hours. The whey separates from the rest of the yogurt leaving you with a thick and creamy Greek-style yogurt for half the price of the ones you find in the store.

# Green Salad with Herbed Buttermilk Ranch Dressing

**Makes 8 side-dish servings or 4 main-dish servings.**

*Compared with bottled dressings, any salad topping you can make at home will be bursting with flavor, encouraging you to dig into your next salad. The mixture of herbs in this recipe is classic for ranch dressing, but feel free to experiment with different herbs to suit your personal taste. To create an entrée from this salad, top with roast chicken or grilled fish.*

## Ingredients

1 cup buttermilk

1 cup mayonnaise

½ cup sour cream or whole-milk Greek-style yogurt

2 tablespoons fresh lemon juice

1 tablespoon Dijon mustard

½ teaspoon garlic powder

1 teaspoon salt

½ teaspoon ground black pepper

Pinch dried hot chili powder (optional)

1 teaspoon dried chives

1 teaspoon dried basil

1 teaspoon dried dill

1 teaspoon dried thyme

2 heads butter lettuce, washed, dried, and torn into bite-sized pieces

1 pint cherry or grape tomatoes, washed and halved

1 cucumber, peeled, seeded, and sliced into half-moons

½ small red onion, sliced into thin half-moons

½ cup shredded carrots

**1.** Make dressing: Place buttermilk, mayonnaise, sour cream, lemon juice, mustard, and garlic powder into the bowl of a blender. Process until smooth. Season to taste with salt, pepper, and hot pepper (if using). Transfer to a bowl and stir in chives, basil, dill, and thyme. Cover and chill until flavors meld and herbs soften, about 20 minutes.

**2.** Arrange lettuce on a large platter or in a salad bowl. Top with tomatoes, cucumber, red onions, and carrots. Serve with dressing.

# Green Mango Salad with Dried Shrimp

**Makes 8 servings.**

*Sweet-sour and slightly spicy, this salad is a showstopper that really comes together with the addition of dried shrimp. You may have had similar salads in Southeast Asian restaurants, where it may be topped with chopped salted peanuts. This version is more traditional, however, and brings umami taste to the salad, rather than the saltiness that peanuts bring.*

## Ingredients

¼ cup fresh lime juice

1 tablespoon fish sauce

2 tablespoons or more brown sugar

1 teaspoon dried ginger powder

½ teaspoon dried garlic powder

1 tablespoon dried basil (preferably Thai basil)

2 green (unripe) mangoes or ½ green papaya

¼ cup red onions, cut into thin half-moons

½ cup cilantro, coarsely chopped

½ cup dried shrimp, minced

½ teaspoon dried chili powder

**1.** Make dressing: Mix lime juice, fish sauce, brown sugar, ginger, garlic, and basil.

**2.** Peel mangoes and remove flesh from pit. Cut into julienne strips using a mandoline, the largest holes on a box grater, or a sharp knife. (If using papaya, peel papaya, remove and discard seeds, and grate flesh on the largest holes of a box grater.) Transfer mango to a large bowl and add onions.

**3.** Toss mango and onions with dressing. Taste mango with dressing, adding more sugar if necessary. (The greenest mangoes are also the most sour, and may require extra sugar.)

**4.** Serve salad topped with cilantro, dried shrimp, and chili powder.

# Pico de Gallo Quinoa Salad

**Makes 8 servings.**

*Bursting with flavor, this salad draws on the staples of Mexican pico de gallo—tomatoes, lime juice, onions, and cilantro—and brings in quinoa, a South American grain. If you like spice, crush a dried small pepper over this salad to really bring the dish together.*

## Ingredients

½ cup dried corn

½ cup dried bell peppers

1 cup uncooked quinoa

¼ cup red onions, diced

3 plum tomatoes, diced

3 tablespoons lime juice

3 tablespoons canola oil

½ teaspoon cumin

¼ cup cilantro, chopped

1 small dried chili pepper or 3 slices dried jalapeño pepper, optional

1–2 teaspoons salt

**1.** Rinse corn and peppers in a mesh strainer and transfer to a medium bowl. Cover with hot water and soak until vegetables are softened, about 20 minutes.

**2.** While vegetables soften, rinse quinoa in a mesh strainer until water runs clear. Cook according to package directions. Drain quinoa and rinse under cold water until room temperature.

**3.** Drain corn and peppers.

**4.** Mix drained quinoa, peppers, and corn in a large bowl. Add onions, tomatoes, lime juice, canola oil, cumin, and cilantro. If using, crush optional peppers over salad. Season to taste with 1 teaspoon salt, adding more if necessary.

**5.** Serve chilled or at room temperature.

## Toasting Quinoa

Depending on the brand, some quinoa has a bitter-tasting coating which is actually a bug repellent. Washing it thoroughly can eliminate some of this but one way to ensure a great-tasting dish every time is to toast it for a few minutes over medium-high heat before boiling.

# Sweet and Sour Kale Salad with Dried Cherries

**Makes 4 servings.**

*Those who have heard about the health benefits of kale but haven't quite found a way to enjoy it should take a chance with this salad. Massaging the kale with salt not only softens its texture but also helps to release some of the bitterness in the greens. The dried cherries stand out beautifully against the vibrant green kale, making this salad an eye-catching dish to add to your next buffet.*

## Ingredients

1 bunch kale

1 teaspoon salt, divided, plus more for sprinkling

¼ cup pine nuts

¼ cup (4 tablespoons) extra-virgin olive oil

Juice from 1 lemon

4–6 teaspoons honey

½ teaspoon ground black pepper

½ cup dried cherries or dried sweetened cranberries

**1.** Wash kale under cool running water and towel dry. Separate leaves from the kale ribs. Discard ribs or use for vegetable stock. Stack up the kale leaves and slice into thin ribbons.

**2.** Place kale in a large bowl. Sprinkle with ½ teaspoon salt and knead the kale until it softens and releases its liquid. Drain kale well and place in a serving bowl.

**3.** Heat a medium skillet over medium-high heat. Add pine nuts and toast, stirring frequently, until golden brown, about 5 minutes. Immediately transfer to a clean plate.

**4.** Make dressing: Mix oil, lemon juice, and 4 teaspoons honey.

**5.** Toss kale with dressing. Add more honey, if desired, and season to taste with salt and pepper. Sprinkle with dried cherries and toasted pine nuts. Serve immediately.

### Mini Me

While kale contains lots of good things like iron, some people just can't bring themselves to eat it. One way to compromise is to try the new baby kale micro greens that many growers, especially organic farmers, are now producing. They're miniature leaves that have the distinctive curly-edge look of their larger counterparts but don't have its bitter and chewy characteristics. The best way to eat them is in a salad with other nutritional powerhouses like spinach.

# White Bean and Haricots Verts Salad with Dried Chive and Dried Lemon Vinaigrette

**Makes 4 servings.**

*The combination of slender green beans, white beans, and red onions will not only delight your eyes, it also brings wonderful flavor and texture combinations to your palate. A deceptively simple dressing gets an extra flavor boost from dried lemon and dried chives. The dressing is also terrific as a topping for roasted beets.*

## Ingredients

1 pound haricots verts (thin green beans), ends trimmed

1 teaspoon salt, divided

½ cup extra-virgin olive oil

3 tablespoons fresh lemon juice

1 teaspoon dried chives

1 teaspoon dried lemon, finely chopped

¼ teaspoon pepper

1 cup cooked white beans, rinsed and drained

¼ cup red onion, minced

**1.** Bring a large pot of water to a boil over high heat. Add ½ teaspoon salt and bring to a boil again. Add haricots verts and boil, uncovered, until bright green and cooked through, about 4 minutes.

**2.** Drain haricots verts and rinse under cold water or plunge into ice water until cold, about 10 minutes.

**3.** Make dressing: Mix oil, lemon juice, chives, dried lemon, remaining ½ teaspoon salt, and pepper until combined. Set aside.

**4.** Drain haricots verts well and transfer to a large bowl. Add white beans, red onion, and dressing and toss to coat vegetables with vinaigrette. Serve.

### Simple Solution

Don't worry if you want to make this dish and can't find haricots verts. Buy regular green beans and slice them into three vertical sections.

# Mushroom Pâté

**Makes 4 servings.**

*Starting a meal with a vegetable pâté is a great way to elevate your dining experience. It's tasty with crackers, dried fruit, or on a bed of lettuce. You can also substitute this pâté for the filling in the palmier recipe featured in Chapter 8.*

## Ingredients

1 cup dried mixed mushrooms

3–4 dried tomatoes

½ slice dried lemon, crumbled

4 ounces cream cheese

1 tablespoon extra-virgin olive oil

1 tablespoon soy sauce or tamari

1 teaspoon lemon juice

1 teaspoon dried thyme or dried rosemary

Pinch ground dried hot pepper

½ teaspoon salt

Assorted crackers or toast points

**1.** Place mushrooms, tomatoes, and lemon into a wire mesh strainer and rinse well. Transfer to a medium bowl and cover with hot water by ½". Soak until softened, about 20 minutes. Drain well.

**2.** Transfer vegetables and lemon to the bowl of a food processor or blender. Add cream cheese, oil, soy sauce, lemon juice, thyme or rosemary, and hot pepper. Pulse ingredients together until roughly combined, then purée until smooth.

**3.** Season to taste with salt.

**4.** Transfer to a small serving bowl, cover, and chill until firm, about 30 minutes. Serve with crackers or toast points.

# CHAPTER 10

# Main Dishes

The dinner table is really dried foods' time to shine. Dried fruits add complexity to savory dishes, while dried vegetables add nutrition to entrées. And the texture of dried foods really bring a bit of intrigue to most familiar dinner foods.

# Chicken Breasts with Goat Cheese and Dried Apricots

**Makes 4 servings.**

*Boneless skinless chicken breasts get a tasty makeover with goat cheese and dried apricots. The creamy and sweet filling really makes the chicken taste meatier, and is enhanced by a glaze that contains apricots, cinnamon, and a touch of spice.*

## Ingredients

4 ounces goat cheese, softened

6 dried apricot halves, minced

4 boneless, skinless chicken breasts

½ teaspoon salt

1 teaspoon rice vinegar

3 tablespoons apricot preserves

½ teaspoon ground cinnamon

¼ teaspoon dried hot pepper flakes

1 tablespoon olive oil

1. Preheat oven to 350°F.
2. Mix goat cheese and apricots together until well combined.
3. Season chicken on both sides with salt.
4. Using a sharp knife, cut a 2" long by 1" deep slit into the side of each chicken breast. Stuff each slit with ¼ of apricot mixture. Secure each slit with a toothpick to keep apricot mixture enclosed in meat.
5. Make glaze: Mix together vinegar, preserves, cinnamon, and red pepper flakes. Set aside.
6. Heat oil in a large skillet over medium-high heat. Add chicken breasts in a single layer and cook until brown, about 6 minutes. Turn chicken and brown on the second side, about 5 minutes.
7. Transfer chicken to a baking sheet and brush each piece with ¼ of the glaze. Bake in the oven until the internal temperature of the chicken reaches 145°F on a meat thermometer, about 15 minutes. Let chicken rest 5 minutes before serving.

# Blood Orange–Glazed Game Hens with Dried Cherry and Wild Rice Stuffing

**Makes 4 servings.**

*If you're looking for suggestions for your next dinner party, you can't go wrong with stuffed game hens. Individually portioned, they make for a dramatic plating. And the combination of dried fruit and blood oranges will have your guests raving.*

## Ingredients

½ cup uncooked white rice

½ cup uncooked wild rice (may substitute 1 cup of wild rice blend for the white rice and wild rice)

1 leek

2 tablespoons unsalted butter

1 clove garlic, minced

½ teaspoon ground dried ginger

½ cup dried cherries (may substitute dried cranberries, raisins, or chopped dried apricots)

1 teaspoon salt, divided

4 Cornish game hens

2 blood oranges

1 star anise

1 tablespoon honey

1. Preheat oven to 375°F.

2. Prepare white rice and wild rice according to package directions. Drain both rices and place in a large bowl.

3. Remove root end from leek and split lengthwise. Rinse leek under cold running water, separating layers to remove any grit that accumulates there. Chop leeks where the tops become dark green. Discard tops of leek (or reserve for another use). Cut remaining white and light green part of leek into ¼" half-moons.

4. Heat medium skillet over medium heat. Add butter and melt. Add leeks and cook, stirring occasionally, until soft and translucent, about 5 minutes. Add garlic and cook until fragrant, an additional 30 seconds. Transfer to bowl with rice. Add ginger, cherries, and ½ teaspoon salt. Mix well.

5. Rinse hens and pat dry. Season all over with remaining salt. Fill each hen with the rice mixture and place hens onto a rack in a roasting pan.

6. Roast hens until they register 140°F on a digital thermometer, about 45 minutes. Remove from oven.

7. As hens roast, make glaze: Using a microplane or the finest setting on a grater, zest both oranges and set aside zest. Juice both oranges into a small saucepan. Add star anise and bring to a boil over medium heat. Simmer until juice reduces by half, about 5 minutes. Remove from heat, remove star anise, and stir in reserved zest and honey.

8. Brush hens with glaze and return to oven. Roast an additional 5 minutes and remove from oven. Let rest 5 minutes and serve.

# Beef with Dried Brandied Cherries

**Makes 4 servings.**

*This elegant, French-inspired dinner brings together tangy-sweet dried cherries with brandy, red wine, dried tarragon, and dried chives. The tarragon offers a flavor that's similar to licorice, which perfectly complements the richness of the steak and its sauce. Delicious served over mashed potatoes, or even with mushroom risotto.*

## Ingredients

½ cup dried cherries

1 cup brandy

4 (6- to 8-ounce) filet mignons

½ teaspoon salt

¼ teaspoon ground black pepper

4 tablespoons unsalted butter, divided into 1-tablespoon pats

2 cups dry red wine

½ teaspoon dried tarragon

1 teaspoon dried chives

**1.** Place cherries into a wire mesh strainer. Rinse under cold running water. Place into a heatproof bowl. Bring brandy to a boil. Allow to cool 1 minute and pour over cherries. Soak until cherries soften, about 20 minutes. Drain cherries, reserving brandy for another use.

**2.** Preheat oven to 400°F.

**3.** Season beef filets on both sides with salt and pepper.

**4.** Heat a large skillet over high heat. Melt 1 tablespoon butter and add steaks. Cook until each steak is dark brown on each side, about 4 minutes per side. Transfer steaks to a baking sheet and bake until steaks are desired doneness, about 3 minutes for rare, 5 minutes for medium, or 7 minutes for well-done. Remove steaks from oven and allow to rest 5 minutes before serving.

**5.** While steaks roast, return skillet to heat. Add wine, tarragon, and chives and boil until liquid is as thick as honey, about 5 minutes. Remove skillet from heat and add remaining butter, one pat at a time, stirring until butter is melted before adding the next pat. Stir in brandied cherries. Season to taste with salt and pepper.

**6.** Serve each steak with equal portions of sauce.

# Braised Beef Brisket with Dried Plums, Apricots, and Garlic

**Makes 8 servings.**

*Many traditional brisket recipes call for a sweet and sour sauce. And how better to achieve the balance of sweetness than through adding your own dried fruit? Plums bring a honeyed sweetness and apricots provide just the right amount of sour. This dish is even better the day after you make it. If possible, prepare one day, refrigerate the brisket, and then bring it to piping hot on the stove right before you serve it.*

## Ingredients

1 (3½–4 pound) brisket, trimmed

1 teaspoon salt

½ teaspoon black pepper

2 tablespoons olive oil

1 (12-ounce) bottle beer

1½ cups orange juice

½ cup dried plums

½ cup dried apricots

3 cloves garlic, peeled

- - - - - - - - - - - - - - - - - - - - - - - - - - - - - - - - - - - - - - - - - - - - - - - - - - - - - - - - - - - - - - - - - - - - - -

**1.** Preheat oven to 225°F.

**2.** Pat excess juices off brisket with paper toweling. Season brisket on both sides with salt and pepper.

**3.** Heat oil in a large Dutch oven over medium-high heat until oil is hot but not smoking, about 3 minutes.

**4.** Add brisket and cook until deep brown on one side, about 8 minutes. Using heavy tongs, flip brisket and cook until the other side is deep brown, about 8 minutes.

**5.** Add beer and orange juice and bring to a boil. Immediately remove from heat.

**6.** Add plums, apricots, and garlic. Cover top of Dutch oven with foil and place lid of Dutch oven onto the pot. Place in oven and roast until brisket is very tender, about 6–7 hours.

**7.** Transfer brisket to a platter and tent loosely with foil.

**8.** Strain cooking liquid. Set solids aside and return liquid to the pot. Bring to a boil over medium-high heat and cook until liquid reduces by half and is as thick as honey, about 10 minutes. Season to taste with salt and pepper, and return strained solids to pan.

**9.** Slice brisket across the grain, and serve with sauce.

# Lamb Stew with Dried Plums

**Makes 6 servings.**

*With deep flavors that result from hours of slowly cooking in your oven, this lamb stew is destined to become one of your favorites. The dried plums melt into a silky sauce and along with the addition of baking spices, heighten the flavor of the lamb.*

## Ingredients

3 pounds lamb (from the shoulder or a boneless leg), cut into 1½" pieces

1 teaspoon salt

½ teaspoon pepper

¼ cup vegetable oil

1 large onion, cut into 1" cubes

2 carrots, peeled and cut into 1" pieces

2 stalks celery, cut into 1" pieces

2 cloves garlic, minced

½ cup flour

4 cups low-sodium beef broth

2 cups dry red wine

½ cup dried plums

½ teaspoon ground allspice

¼ teaspoon ground cloves

Pinch cayenne pepper

**1.** Place oven rack on the lowest rung of your oven, ensuring there is enough clearance above it to place a large Dutch oven. Preheat oven to 225°F.

**2.** Sprinkle lamb with salt and pepper.

**3.** Heat a large, heavy Dutch oven over medium-high heat. Add oil. When hot but not smoking, cook the lamb in 3–4 batches until well browned on all sides, about 8–10 minutes. Transfer cooked lamb to a large bowl and set aside. Repeat for remaining lamb.

**4.** Add onions, carrots, and celery to pot, and cook, stirring frequently, until vegetables are slightly browned and a little softened, about 5 minutes. Add garlic and cook until garlic is fragrant, about 30 seconds.

**5.** Add flour and cook, stirring constantly, until lightly toasted, about 2 minutes. Add broth, wine, dried plums, allspice, cloves, and cayenne and bring to a boil. Add meat to pot, cover, and transfer to oven. Cook until meat is tender, about 3 hours.

**6.** Season to taste with salt and pepper and serve over cooked wild rice.

# Spice and Chili–Rubbed Pulled Pork

**Makes 8 servings.**

*Your own dried garlic, lemon, thyme, and chilies come together with a vibrant mixture of spices to create a rich and complex pulled pork. Rather than smoking the meat over a grill, this recipe relies on a low oven, meaning you can serve pulled pork any time of the year. This dish freezes and reheats well, so make extra.*

## Ingredients

1 tablespoon dried garlic powder

½ teaspoon dried lemon powder

1 tablespoon dried thyme

2 teaspoons dried chili pepper powder

1 teaspoon ground cumin

2 teaspoons ground black pepper

1 teaspoon salt

1 teaspoon brown sugar

1 teaspoon dry mustard

1 (4-pound) pork shoulder

2 tablespoons vegetable oil or melted bacon grease

2 cups apple cider

2 cups dry white wine

**1.** Preheat oven to 225°F.

**2.** Combine garlic powder, lemon powder, thyme, chili powder, cumin, pepper, salt, brown sugar, and mustard in a small bowl.

**3.** Remove pork from its packaging and pat dry with paper towels. Sprinkle all over with spice mixture.

**4.** Heat oil in a large Dutch oven over medium-high heat until oil is hot but not smoking, about 3 minutes.

**5.** Add pork and cook until deep brown on all sides, about 5 minutes per side. Add cider and white wine and bring to a boil. Immediately remove from heat.

**6.** Cover Dutch oven with a tight-fitting lid and place in oven. Roast until pork pulls apart easily, about 6 hours.

**7.** Remove pork from oven and remove lid from Dutch oven. Allow pork to cool to room temperature in its own juices, about 45 minutes. Using two forks, shred the meat into bite-sized pieces.

**8.** To serve, heat meat in its own juice on the stovetop. Serve with your favorite barbecue sauce.

# Cod with Spicy Tomato Sauce Accented with Cauliflower and Golden Raisins

**Makes 4 servings.**

*Roasted cod topped with a tomato sauce is terrific any time of the year. The combination of cauliflower sautéed until golden, chili flakes, and golden raisins works well with any moist fish. So if you're not a fan of cod, substitute sea bass, halibut, or barramundi.*

## Ingredients

2 tablespoons extra-virgin olive oil

1 clove garlic, minced

½ teaspoon crushed red pepper flakes

2 cups cauliflower, shredded

1 (28-ounce) can crushed tomatoes

½ cup golden raisins

1 teaspoon sea salt

½ teaspoon ground pepper

4 large cod fillets

**1.** Heat olive oil over medium heat in a large, heavy saucepan. Add garlic and red pepper flakes and sauté until fragrant, about 30 seconds.

**2.** Add cauliflower and sauté until deep golden brown, stirring frequently, about 10–12 minutes.

**3.** Add crushed tomatoes and bring to a boil. Stir in raisins. Reduce heat to low and simmer, uncovered, 60–90 minutes.

**4.** Season with salt and ground pepper. Add more to taste, if necessary.

**5.** Preheat oven to 400°F. Pat cod dry with paper towels and place in a single layer on a baking sheet. Season with salt and pepper. Bake 8–10 minutes until fish flakes easily and is solid white.

**6.** Place cod onto plates and divide sauce evenly. Top each fish fillet with sauce.

# Grilled Tuna with Papaya Chutney

**Makes 4 servings.**

*Any time you have dried papaya in your cabinets, you can have a Hawaiian-inspired dinner in minutes. The dried papaya softens in vegetable oil and lime juice in the time it takes to sear the tuna steaks. And if you're not in the mood for tuna, this chutney works well on any fish, or is even a terrific topper for corn chips.*

## Ingredients

⅔ cup dried papaya, chopped into ¼" pieces

¼ cup dried green onions, diced

1 small or ½ large dried chili pepper (optional)

¼ cup chopped fresh cilantro

4 tablespoons vegetable oil, divided

2 tablespoons fresh lime juice

1 teaspoon grated lime zest

4 (6-ounce) fresh tuna steaks

½ teaspoon salt

¼ teaspoon black pepper

**1.** Make papaya chutney: Combine papaya, onions, peppers (if using), cilantro, 3 tablespoons oil (1 tablespoon should remain), lime juice, and lime zest in a small bowl. Set aside.

**2.** Preheat grill to high. Brush tuna steaks on both sides with remaining oil. Season tuna with salt and pepper on both sides.

**3.** Grill tuna until golden brown on one side, about 3–4 minutes. Flip and grill second side until golden brown on the second side, about 2–3 minutes. Tuna should still be medium-rare on the inside. Remove tuna from grill and top with relish.

# Shrimp Stir-Fry with Dried Cabbage and Dried Broccoli

**Makes 4 servings.**

*Perfect for a quick dinner, this Cantonese-style stir-fry comes together really quickly because of the dried cabbage. While you're softening the cabbage, you can make the sauce and prep the shrimp. Because the cabbage is pre-sliced and has a controlled amount of water, all it takes is a quick warm-up in oil, a few minutes of sautéing shrimp, and dinner is done. Dehydrated broccoli makes for a crunchy garnish for the stir-fry, rather than your traditional sesame seed topping.*

## Ingredients

1½ cups dried cabbage

½ cup water

2 tablespoons rice wine or dry sherry

1 teaspoon sesame oil

1 teaspoon cornstarch

½ teaspoon dried ginger powder

¼ teaspoon ground black pepper

1 tablespoon vegetable oil

1 clove garlic, minced

½ teaspoon salt, divided

1 pound shrimp, peeled and deveined

¼ cup dried broccoli

2 scallions, thinly sliced

2 cups cooked rice or cooked Asian noodles

**1.** Place cabbage in a wire mesh strainer. Rinse under cold, running water. Transfer to a medium bowl and cover with hot water. Soak until softened, about 10 minutes. Drain and set aside.

**2.** Place water, rice wine, sesame oil, cornstarch, ginger, and pepper in a small bowl. Stir to combine and place next to the stove.

**3.** Heat 1 tablespoon oil in a large skillet over medium-high heat. When oil is hot but not smoking, add garlic and stir until fragrant, about 30 seconds. Add cabbage, sprinkle with a pinch of salt, and cook, stirring frequently, until cabbage heats through, about 2 minutes.

**4.** Add shrimp and continue to cook, stirring frequently, until shrimp turns pink, about 3 minutes. Add sauce and stir until thickened, about 2 minutes. Season to taste with remaining salt.

**5.** Sprinkle with dried broccoli and scallions. Serve stir-fry over rice or noodles.

# Baked Falafel with Tahini-Mint Dressing

**Makes 4 servings.**

*A Middle Eastern staple, falafel is deceptively simple to prepare at home, especially this baked version. Your own dried garlic and mint give the chickpea fritters impact, while dried mint also enhances the creamy dipping sauce. Falafel is great served in a pita with lettuce and tomatoes; it's also delicious served atop a green salad.*

## Ingredients

½ cup tahini

2 cloves garlic

1 teaspoon salt, divided

¼ cup fresh lemon juice

¼ cup olive oil

2 tablespoons or more water

1½ teaspoons dried mint, divided

1½ cups cooked chickpeas, rinsed and drained

3 pieces dried garlic, or 1 teaspoon garlic powder

1½ teaspoons cumin powder

½ teaspoon black pepper

½ teaspoon baking soda

2 tablespoons chickpea flour, rice flour, or cornstarch

Pan spray or 1 tablespoon olive oil

1. Make Tahini-Mint Dressing: Stir tahini within its container to blend the paste and the oil (tahini separates during storage). Measure stirred tahini into the bowl of a food processor or blender. Add garlic, ½ teaspoon salt, lemon juice, and olive oil. Purée until well blended. If too thick, add water 1 tablespoon at a time and blend until it reaches desired consistency. Stir in 1 teaspoon mint and set sauce aside.

2. Preheat oven to 400°F.

3. Place chickpeas, dried garlic, remaining mint, cumin, remaining ½ teaspoon salt, pepper, baking soda, and flour into the bowl of a food processor. Process until smooth and well blended.

4. Divide mixture into 12 equal parts. Roll each part into a 1" ball.

5. Spray a baking sheet with pan spray or brush with oil. Place falafel onto sheet and cook, rolling a quarter-turn every 5 minutes, until golden brown on all sides, about 20–25 minutes.

6. Serve cooked falafel with Tahini-Mint Dressing.

# Black Bean Burgers with Mango Salsa

**Makes 4 servings.**

*The combination of fresh mango with dried mango makes for a salsa that is anything but traditional. Sweet with just a hint of tanginess and a pleasantly chewy texture, this salsa brings out the earthiness in the bean burgers. It's also delicious on grilled chicken thighs.*

## Ingredients

½ cup dried mango, cut into ¼" dice

½ teaspoon dried jalapeño powder

1 fresh mango, peeled, seeded, and cut into ¼" dice

2 tablespoons red onion, finely diced

Juice of ½ lime or more to taste

2 tablespoons chopped fresh cilantro

½ teaspoon salt, divided

¼ cup dried bell pepper

3 cups cooked black beans, rinsed and drained

1 teaspoon dried chili powder

1 teaspoon dried garlic powder

1½ teaspoons ground cumin

6 tablespoons breadcrumbs (preferably whole wheat), or more

Pan spray or 1 tablespoon vegetable oil

**1.** Make salsa: Stir together dried mango, jalapeño powder, fresh mango, onion, lime juice, cilantro, and a pinch of salt. Taste, adding more lime juice or salt if necessary. Set aside.

**2.** Place bell pepper into a wire mesh strainer and rinse under cold running water. Place into a heatproof bowl and cover with hot water until softened, about 20 minutes. Drain peppers, reserving soaking liquid.

**3.** Place beans, peppers, chili powder, garlic powder, cumin, and breadcrumbs in a medium bowl. Mash with a potato masher. Add ½ teaspoon salt and a squeeze of lime juice and taste. Add more salt if necessary.

**4.** Make a patty with a small amount of the mixture to test for consistency. If mixture is too stiff, add reserved pepper-soaking liquid, 1 tablespoon at a time, until it reaches desired consistency. If mixture is too thin, add more breadcrumbs, 1 tablespoon at a time, until it reaches desired consistency.

**5.** Form four patties from mixture.

**6.** Spray a nonstick skillet with pan spray (or place half of oil in a nonstick skillet) and heat over medium heat until hot but not smoking. Add two burgers and cook until crispy and toasted on one side, about 4 minutes. Flip and cook until other side is crispy and toasted, about 3–4 minutes. Remove from pan and tent with foil to keep warm. Repeat with remaining burgers.

**7.** To serve, place each burger on a plate and top with one-fourth of the salsa.

# Moroccan Tagine with Seven Vegetables

**Makes 8 servings.**

*Moroccans, like Americans, view seven as a lucky number. Therefore, any tagine made with seven distinct vegetables is thought to be a lucky dish. This recipe is a hearty vegetarian stew. If you would like to make a version with meat, add 3 cups of cubed cooked chicken or turkey when you add the raisins and tomatoes.*

## Ingredients

2 pounds eggplant, cut into 1" cubes

1½ teaspoons sea or kosher salt, divided

2 tablespoons olive oil

1 medium yellow or white onion, cut into ½" dice

3 cloves garlic, minced

3 cups low-sodium vegetable broth

1 cinnamon stick, 2"–3" long

½ teaspoon ginger powder

½ teaspoon paprika

1 teaspoon ground cumin

½ teaspoon turmeric

2 carrots, peeled and cut into ¼" rounds

1 zucchini, peeled and cut into ¼" rounds

½ cup dried red bell pepper

1 (15-ounce) can cooked chickpeas, drained and rinsed

2 plum tomatoes, cored and cut into ½" dice

¼ cup golden raisins

¼ cup dried pitted dates, cut into ¼" slices

2 tablespoons chopped cilantro, separated

½ teaspoon fresh ground pepper

2 cups cooked couscous

**1.** Place eggplant in a colander and sprinkle with ½ teaspoon salt. Toss well and let drain 20 minutes. Rinse, pat dry with a paper towel, and set aside.

**2.** Heat oil in a Dutch oven over medium heat. Add onion and eggplant and sauté until vegetables soften, about 5–10 minutes. Add garlic and sauté until fragrant, about 30 seconds.

**3.** Stir in broth, spices, carrots, zucchini, and red pepper. Bring to a boil, reduce heat, and simmer, uncovered, for 15 minutes.

**4.** Stir in chickpeas, tomatoes, raisins, dates, half of cilantro, remaining 1 teaspoon salt, and pepper. Simmer, covered, for 10 minutes.

**5.** Serve atop cooked couscous, sprinkled with remaining cilantro.

# Mushroom Stroganoff with Dill

**Makes 4 servings.**

*For a hearty vegetarian meal, you can't go wrong with mushroom stroganoff. The intense flavor of dried mushrooms combines with a silky sauce to satisfy the largest of appetites. And if you prefer, you may add filet mignon to this dish. You'll also find that it's a great dinner for post-Thanksgiving, as you can stir cooked turkey into the dish instead of beef.*

## Ingredients

2 cups dried mixed mushrooms

1–2 tablespoons unsalted butter

1 large onion, sliced into thin half-moons

2 filets mignons, sliced into long, thin strips
   (optional)

1 teaspoon dried dill

½ teaspoon dried garlic powder

¾ cup sour cream

1 teaspoon lemon juice

½ teaspoon salt

¼ teaspoon pepper

**1.** Rinse and drain mushrooms. Place in a large bowl and cover with warm water. Soak until mushrooms are softened, 20 minutes. Drain, reserving soaking liquid.

**2.** Heat a large pan over medium-high heat. Add 1 tablespoon butter and onions. Cook, stirring frequently, until onions are translucent, about 6–8 minutes.

**3.** Add mushrooms and cook until they begin to brown, 2–3 minutes. Transfer mixture to a large bowl.

**4.** If using steak, return pan to stove and turn heat to high. Add remaining butter and half of filet strips to pan in a single layer. Cook until filet is brown on both sides, 1–2 minutes per side. Transfer filet to a baking sheet and repeat with remaining filet strips.

**5.** Return empty pan to stove and turn heat to high. Add reserved mushroom-soaking liquid, dill, and garlic powder, and cook until liquid has reduced to 2 tablespoons, about 4–5 minutes.

**6.** Return onions, mushrooms, and filet to pan. Add sour cream, lemon, salt, and pepper. Cook until heated through and flavors combine, about 1 minute.

# CHAPTER 11
# Sides

Turn your side dishes into the most interesting part of any meal with flavorful dehydrated foods. Whether you're looking for the savory kick of dried meat or fish, a touch of sweetness from dried fruit, or a quick flavor punch from dried cheese or vegetables, you'll find that dehydrated foods are the secret ingredient that will make your side dishes sing.

# Asian Green Beans with Dried Shrimp

**Makes 4 servings.**

*These blistered green beans with an Asian sauce full of heat will make you think you've ordered in from your favorite Chinese takeout. Dried shrimp take green beans from an ordinary side dish to a restaurant-quality one. Use this recipe to round out an Asian meal, or serve with simple baked fish and steamed rice.*

## Ingredients

2 tablespoons vegetable oil, divided

1 pound green beans, trimmed and cut into 1½" pieces

2 tablespoons soy sauce

½ teaspoon dried ginger powder

1 teaspoon sugar

1 tablespoon Chinese rice wine or sherry

2 scallions, minced

2 tablespoons dried shrimp, minced

3–4 dried whole chili peppers, or to taste

1 clove garlic, smashed

**1.** Heat 1 tablespoon oil in a large skillet or wok over high heat. When oil is hot but not smoking, add green beans and cook, stirring constantly, until green beans soften and are lightly charred, 7–8 minutes. Remove from pan and set aside.

**2.** Whisk together soy sauce, ginger, sugar, rice wine, and scallions. Keep mixture close to the stove.

**3.** Return skillet to stove and heat remaining oil on high heat. When oil is hot but not smoking, add dried shrimp, dried chili peppers, and garlic. Cook, stirring constantly, until garlic is golden, about 45 seconds. Immediately add green beans and sauce and mix well. Cook 1 minute to thicken sauce and serve.

# Baked Beans

**Makes 8 servings.**

*The perfect addition to any barbecue, baked beans are a great way to show off the difference between homemade dried powders (like ginger and garlic) and those purchased in stores. You'll see in this recipe how you're able to use smaller quantities of your own powders as compared to commercially produced powders.*

## Ingredients

1 pound dried navy, butter, or pinto beans

2 pieces bacon, cooked and crumbled

6 cups water

½ cup dehydrated onion

½ teaspoon dried garlic powder

½ teaspoon dried ginger powder

1 teaspoon dry mustard

¼ teaspoon whole cloves

¼ teaspoon allspice berries

½ cup molasses

1 tablespoon cider vinegar

1 teaspoon salt

½ teaspoon ground black pepper

Pinch dried hot pepper powder

**1.** Place beans in a wire mesh strainer and rinse under cold running water. Transfer to a large bowl and cover with cold water by 2". Soak 8–12 hours. Alternately, quick-soak beans: Bring beans, covered by 2" of water, to a boil. Boil, uncovered, 2 minutes. Turn off heat and let beans soak 1 hour.

**2.** Preheat oven to 350°F.

**3.** Drain beans and transfer to a large Dutch oven with bacon, water, onion, garlic powder, ginger powder, mustard, cloves, allspice, and molasses. Cover pot and bake until beans are tender, about 4–6 hours.

**4.** Transfer beans to stovetop and place over medium heat. Remove lid and simmer until most of liquid is absorbed. Stir in vinegar, salt, pepper, and hot pepper powder. Simmer an additional 10 minutes, correcting seasoning if necessary.

### Take It Slow

You can also make beans in a slow cooker. Cook on high 4–6 hours until beans are tender.

# Corn Gratin with Roasted Poblano Peppers

**Makes 8 servings.**

*This creamy side dish gets its intense flavors from roasted poblano peppers, which are slightly spicier than a bell pepper, and both dried and fresh corn. It's delicious with the crunchy topping or without, if you prefer a gluten-free treat. And if you'd like to turn this side into a main dish, simply add chopped cooked chicken or turkey.*

## Ingredients

3 fresh poblano peppers

1½ cups heavy cream or half-and-half

½ teaspoon dried garlic powder

1 cup dried corn kernels

1 teaspoon salt

1 teaspoon unsalted butter or pan spray

2 cups fresh corn kernels

1 cup shredded mild cheese, such as Chihuahua, Monterey jack, or mild Cheddar

1 cup breadcrumbs or 1 cup crushed corn chips

**1.** Preheat oven to 350°F.

**2.** Place poblano peppers directly onto a gas burner (either on your grill or stove) and turn flame on high. Roast peppers until black on one side, about 6–8 minutes. Carefully turn peppers with metal tongs and roast on other side until black, about 6–8 minutes. Transfer peppers to a brown paper bag, and roll bag to close tightly. Let stand 15 minutes.

**3.** Remove peppers from paper bag and run under cold water. Rub skins off peppers with your hands. Remove stems and seeds from peppers and discard. Cut peppers into ½" pieces.

**4.** Place cream, garlic powder, and dried corn in a medium saucepan. Bring to a boil and stir in salt.

**5.** Butter a 2-quart shallow baking dish. Sprinkle fresh corn into dish in an even layer. Top with pepper pieces. Pour cream mixture over to coat evenly. Cover dish with foil and bake 45 minutes.

**6.** Turn off oven and preheat broiler to high.

**7.** Mix together cheese and breadcrumbs. Remove foil from gratin and sprinkle with breadcrumb-cheese mixture. Place under broiler and cook until breadcrumbs are toasted and cheese is melted, about 3 minutes. Remove from broiler and let rest 5 minutes before serving.

# Dried Apple and Aged Cheddar Beggar's Purses

**Makes 12 pieces, enough for 12 side-dish servings.**

*The combination of dried apples, raisins, Cheddar cheese, and phyllo dough makes beggar's purses taste like a cheese course in a few bites. If your grocer doesn't carry frozen phyllo dough, you can substitute frozen puff pastry dough or wonton wrappers.*

## Ingredients

½ cup dried apples, chopped

¼ cup raisins

¾ cup shredded aged white Cheddar cheese

12 sheets frozen phyllo dough, thawed, wrapped in plastic to keep moist

4 tablespoons unsalted butter, melted

1. Preheat oven to 375°F.
2. Place apples and raisins in a wire mesh strainer. Rinse under cold running water. Transfer to a small bowl and cover with hot water. Soak until fruit is soft, about 10 minutes.
3. Drain fruit well and thoroughly mix with Cheddar cheese.
4. Place phyllo dough on a work surface and remove from plastic. Cover with a clean, damp kitchen towel. Keep phyllo covered as you work.
5. Remove one sheet of phyllo and brush with melted butter. Place a second sheet of phyllo on top of the first and brush with melted butter. Repeat with two additional sheets of phyllo so that you have a stack of four sheets of phyllo.
6. Cut phyllo stack in half lengthwise and then crosswise so you have four stacks.
7. Place 1 rounded teaspoon fruit-Cheddar mixture onto center of each stack and gather the corners together above the filling, pinching where the corners meet to form a seal. Transfer to a baking sheet. Repeat process until you have 12 beggar's purses.
8. Bake until golden brown, about 10–12 minutes.

### An Easy Snack or Appetizer

Pairing cheese and apples is a match made in heaven but there are lots of other combinations you can try in these beggar's purses. Try dried pear with bleu cheese or even mozzarella with sun-dried tomatoes.

# Dried Fruit Medley with Couscous

**Makes 4 servings.**

*This recipe may be the simplest in the book, and is a showcase for the impact of dehydrated fruit on a starchy side dish. Couscous is a Middle Eastern starch that you prepare by steaming in fragrant chicken broth. The addition of sweet fruit, such as raisins and apples, gives a slight sweetness to the dish, and also adds visual appeal.*

## Ingredients

½ cup mixed dried fruits (raisins, dried apples, dried cherries, dried lemons), cut into pieces roughly the size of raisins

1 cup couscous

1 teaspoon salt

1 teaspoon extra-virgin olive oil

3 cups chicken stock or vegetable stock

Plastic wrap

**1.** Place dried fruit into a wire mesh strainer and rinse well under cold running water. Transfer to a medium heatproof bowl.

**2.** Add couscous, salt, and oil. Stir until well mixed.

**3.** Bring stock to a rolling boil. Add water to couscous, stir once to combine, and immediately cover bowl tightly with plastic wrap.

**4.** Let sit until water is absorbed and fruit is softened, about 10 minutes.

**5.** Remove plastic wrap and discard. Fluff couscous with fork and serve.

### Curried Version

A wonderful addition to this dish is some curry powder. Simply add about a tablespoon to the water at the same time as the couscous and enjoy how it intensifies the flavor of the dried fruit.

# Dried Mushroom Risotto

**Makes 4 servings.**

*Risotto is a quintessential Italian dish—starchy Arborio rice simmered with chicken broth and aromatic vegetables, with a quick sprinkling of Parmesan cheese stirred in at the end. By using dried mushrooms instead of fresh, the mushroom flavor is intensified. Italian varieties of mushrooms, such as dried porcinis, give this risotto a true Italian flavor.*

## Ingredients

4–5 cups chicken stock

½ cup dried mushrooms

¼ cup dried English peas (not split peas)

2 tablespoons unsalted butter

1 shallot, finely diced

1 cup Arborio rice

⅓ cup dry white wine

⅓ cup shredded Parmesan cheese

**1.** Place chicken stock in a medium saucepan and bring to a boil. Reduce heat and simmer.

**2.** Rinse mushrooms. Place mushrooms in a small bowl and cover with warm chicken stock (about ½ cup). Rinse peas. Place peas in a second small bowl and cover with warm chicken stock (about ½ cup). Allow vegetables to rehydrate 20–30 minutes.

**3.** Meanwhile, start risotto. Heat a second medium saucepan over medium heat. Add butter and melt.

**4.** Add shallot and cook, stirring occasionally, until shallot is translucent, about 6 minutes.

**5.** Add rice and stir to coat rice with butter and shallot. Add wine and cook, stirring, until all wine is absorbed, about 4 minutes.

**6.** Add 1 cup of stock and stir. Turn heat to low. Cook rice slowly, stirring frequently, until stock is absorbed. Add ½ cup of stock and repeat. Continue adding stock, ½ cup at a time, cooking rice slowly, and stirring frequently, until each ½ cup of stock is absorbed. After you've added about 3 cups of stock, check rice for doneness. Rice should be slightly chewy, but should be cooked through. Continue adding stock slowly until rice is completely cooked.

**7.** Drain mushrooms, reserving liquid. If necessary, slice mushrooms into bite-sized pieces. Add reserved mushroom liquid and mushrooms into risotto, stirring until liquid is fully absorbed.

**8.** Add peas, along with their soaking liquid, into risotto, stirring until liquid is fully absorbed.

**9.** Add cheese and stir until cheese is melted. Serve immediately.

# Edamame Sauté with Dried Tofu, Mushrooms, and Ginger

**Makes 4 side-dish servings or 2 main-dish servings.**

*Boiled soybeans, or edamame, are often thought of as a stand-alone ingredient, but they are terrific when mixed with other flavors. This stir-fry, which boasts your own dried tofu, mushrooms, and ginger powder, is a favorite, and would also make an excellent main dish served over brown rice.*

## Ingredients

¼ cup dried mushrooms, preferably shiitake

¼ cup dried tofu

2 tablespoons soy sauce or tamari

1 tablespoon rice wine or dry sherry

½ cup water

½ teaspoon dried ginger

2 tablespoons vegetable oil

2 cups shelled frozen edamame (soybeans), defrosted

1 red bell pepper, cut into ¼" pieces

1 teaspoon sesame oil

**1.** Place mushrooms in a wire mesh strainer and rinse well under cold running water.

**2.** Transfer to a small pot. Add tofu, soy sauce, rice wine, water, and ginger. Bring to a boil. Remove from heat, cover, and let stand.

**3.** Heat oil in a large, heavy pan over medium-high heat. Add edamame and red peppers and cook, stirring constantly, until peppers are softened and vegetables are starting to brown, about 7 minutes.

**4.** Add mushroom-tofu mixture and cook, stirring constantly, until moisture is absorbed, about 4 minutes. Remove from heat, stir in sesame oil, and serve.

### A Healthy Snack

This dish is not only perfect as a side dish but makes a great snack too. Edamame is high in protein and low in fat. You can find them shelled or in their pods in the frozen food section of most supermarkets. They're ideal for lunch boxes or munching on when you need a quick burst of energy but don't want to spoil your appetite before supper.

# Homemade Hot Sauce

**Makes 2 cups.**

*Although hot sauces are typically made from fresh chili peppers, making hot sauce from dried peppers has its advantages. Stemming and seeding peppers is easier with dried peppers, as they simply snap open, making their seeds quick to remove. Also, the dried product will not change flavor in time, unlike sauces made from fresh peppers.*

## Ingredients

2 loosely packed cups dried hot chili peppers (red, green, or mixed)

½ cup neutral vinegar (such as distilled white, rice, or white wine vinegar)

½ cup water

1 tablespoon sugar

1 teaspoon salt

1 tablespoon canola oil

**1.** Place chili peppers in a wire mesh strainer. Rinse under cold running water.

**2.** Wearing gloves, snap stems off peppers and discard stems. Open peppers lengthwise, remove seeds, and discard seeds. Place seeded peppers into a small saucepan.

**3.** Add remaining ingredients to saucepan. Bring to a boil, then remove from heat. Cover pan and let mixture steep until peppers are soft, about 30 minutes.

**4.** Transfer mixture to the bowl of a blender, food processor, or spice grinder. Purée on high until peppers are completely dissolved, about 4–6 minutes.

**5.** Transfer sauce to a bottle for storage.

### Bring On the Heat

The heat of chili peppers is most concentrated in the stems, ribs, and seeds of the peppers. If you like a very spicy hot sauce, you may leave the peppers intact with stems and seeds.

# Parmesan and Herb–Roasted Potatoes

**Makes 4 servings.**

*Mashed potatoes are a great, standard side dish, but roast potatoes make any meal a bit more refined. Crisp on the outside, with fluffy middles, they are an addicting side dish.*

## Ingredients

2–4 tablespoons olive oil

4 large Yukon gold potatoes, scrubbed and cut into 1" cubes

1 tablespoon dried herbs (basil, thyme, chives, sage, rosemary, oregano, or a combination)

¼ cup grated Parmesan cheese

1 teaspoon salt

½ teaspoon black pepper

**1.** Preheat oven to 325°F.

**2.** Mix 2 tablespoons oil with ingredients together in a large bowl. Toss to coat potatoes completely. If necessary, add more oil to coat.

**3.** Transfer potatoes to a rimmed baking sheet. Bake until potatoes are browned and cooked through, 40–50 minutes. Serve immediately.

### A New Twist for an Old Favorite

If you ever get tired of serving potatoes the same way this is the perfect dish to perk up those spuds. They pair with just about anything from a plain hamburger to a fancy steak. The great thing is you can experiment with what herbs you use and even the cheese. You can add some spices too.

# "Refried" Beans with Dried Red Peppers

**Makes 8 servings.**

*Refried beans are usually made by cooking dried beans and then frying them in lard or vegetable oil. In this healthy and easy version, you cook beans in a slow cooker with the addition of home-dried bell peppers, onions, and garlic, and then mash them into a paste without additional oil. These are great with a grating of a fresh Mexican cheese, such as Chihuahua or Oaxaca.*

## Ingredients

1 pound dried pinto, kidney, or black beans, rinsed well, and checked for stones

8 cups water

½ cup dried red bell peppers

¼ cup dried onion, scallion, or shallot

1 teaspoon dried garlic

1 tablespoon salt

1. Place beans and water in slow cooker. Discard any beans that float.
2. Add water, peppers, onion, and garlic. Stir.
3. Place cover on slow cooker and cook on high until beans are very tender, about 8 hours. Add water to beans if the level of water is lower than ½" above the beans.
4. Add salt and cook 10 minutes. Taste for salt and adjust, if necessary.
5. Strain beans, reserving cooking liquid. Transfer beans to a large bowl and mash with a potato masher, until beans are thoroughly mashed. For a thinner consistency, add bean-cooking liquid ½ cup at a time, until the beans are as thick as you'd like to serve them. Serve immediately.

### An Easy Lunch or Supper

You probably won't have any leftovers after you make this one but if you do try bean and cheese quesadillas. Take ¼ cup of refried beans and spread it between two tortillas, add some shredded cheese, and fry for a few minutes on each side until golden brown. Serve with sour cream and avocado.

# Roasted Carrots and Parsnips with Dried Autumn Fruits

**Makes 4 servings.**

*Root vegetables and fall fruits pair well and make a perfect autumn side dish. Parsnips look like a white carrot, but offer a slightly sweeter and nuttier taste. A spoonful of honey added at the end of this dish brings the flavors together.*

## Ingredients

½ cup dried fall fruit (apples, pears, raisins, dates, or a mixture)

½ pound carrots

½ pound parsnips

2 tablespoons olive oil

½ teaspoon salt

¼ teaspoon pepper

1 tablespoon honey

**1.** Place dried fruit in a small bowl. Cover with warm water and soak until softened, about 10 minutes.

**2.** Preheat oven to 325°F.

**3.** Peel carrots and remove stem ends. Cut into ½"-thick diagonal slices. Repeat with parsnips.

**4.** Drain dried fruit and transfer to a large bowl. Add carrots, parsnips, oil, salt, and pepper. Toss until all vegetables are well coated.

**5.** Transfer to a single layer on a baking sheet. Bake, uncovered, until vegetables are softened and starting to brown, 35–45 minutes.

**6.** Remove from oven, toss with honey, and serve.

### What Shall I Bring?

If you're ever in a dilemma about what to take to the next Thanksgiving gathering, look no further than this dish. It not only tastes good and is easy to put together but it has beautiful colors of the season.

# Sautéed Brussels Sprouts with Raisins, White Wine, and Dijon Mustard

**Makes 4 servings.**

*Herbaceous-tasting Brussels sprouts have a natural affinity for white wine and pungent Dijon mustard. The addition of sweet raisins presents the perfect foil for the richness of the dish, offering just a hint of sweetness in each bite. Also great with other members of the Brassica family, such as broccoli or cabbage.*

## Ingredients

2 tablespoons olive oil

1 pound Brussels sprouts, cleaned, trimmed, and cut into ¼" slices

2 tablespoons dry white wine

¼ cup Dijon mustard

½ cup raisins

½ teaspoon salt

¼ teaspoon pepper

**1.** Heat half of oil in a large, heavy pan over medium-high heat. Add half of Brussels sprouts and cook, stirring frequently, until Brussels sprouts are browned and cooked through, about 8–10 minutes. Transfer to a baking sheet. Add remaining oil and repeat with remaining Brussels sprouts.

**2.** Return all Brussels sprouts to pan. Add wine, mustard, and raisins to pan and stir until well combined. Cook until mixture is thickened, about 2 minutes. Season to taste with salt and pepper.

### Sticky Situation

Some mustards have a tendency to get sticky when heated. If you find that's the case in this dish, simply add some water or chicken or vegetable broth and use it to deglaze the pan so all the flavors, including the mustard, are lifted from the pan and incorporated into the sprouts.

# Southern Macaroni and Cheese

**Makes 8 side-dish, or 4 main-dish, servings.**

*What separates Southern macaroni and cheese from other macaroni and cheese types is the fact that it's covered with a thick layer of crispy breadcrumbs and cheese, whereas other types of mac and cheese don't have the topping. By using dehydrated cheese powder, you'll have a smoother sauce covering the macaroni, but will still have the same great Cheddar taste.*

## Ingredients

1 pound macaroni, fusilli, orecchiette, or shells

6 tablespoons unsalted butter, separated

6 tablespoons flour

6 cups milk

1 bay leaf, whole

1 recipe dehydrated Cheddar cheese, powdered

1 teaspoon dry mustard

Pinch cayenne

¼-½ teaspoon salt

½ teaspoon ground black pepper

½ cup shredded Cheddar cheese

½ cup dry breadcrumbs

**1.** Cook pasta according to package directions. Drain and set aside.

**2.** Place a large, heavy pot over medium heat. Add 5 tablespoons butter and melt. Add flour and cook until flour is lightly toasted, about 2 minutes. Remove pot from heat and slowly whisk in milk, ensuring that the mixture is well blended. Add bay leaf.

**3.** Return pot to medium heat and bring mixture to a simmer. Simmer, stirring frequently, until mixture is thickened, about 20 minutes. Remove from heat and remove bay leaf. Whisk in cheese powder, mustard, and cayenne. Season to taste with salt and pepper.

**4.** Adjust rack to be 3" from broiler. Preheat broiler to medium (or low if medium is not an option).

**5.** Add pasta to cheese sauce and toss well to coat. Transfer mixture to a broiler-safe 13" × 9" × 2" pan.

**6.** Mix shredded Cheddar with reserved butter and breadcrumbs. Sprinkle mixture evenly over pasta. Broil until dish is bubbly and topping is browned, 3–4 minutes. Serve.

### Make Your Own Versions

Nothing says comfort food more than mac and cheese. Best thing is it never has to be boring or the same version twice. Add different cheeses, even a smoked Cheddar or Gouda, or even treats like reconstituted sun-dried tomatoes to the mix.

# Stuffed Green Chilies with Pinto Beans and Dried Fruit

**Makes 4 servings.**

*This Mexican staple is a perfect complement to any main dish. The green poblanos, brick-red filling, cream-colored sauce, and vibrant pomegranate seeds add visual appeal, while the flavor combination of sweet dried summer fruits, earthy beans, and slightly spicy peppers keeps your tastebuds alert. If you prefer a less spicy dish, replace the poblanos with green bell peppers.*

## Ingredients
4 large fresh poblano chili peppers
1 tablespoon vegetable oil
1 teaspoon salt, divided
1 cup walnuts
½ cup half-and-half or heavy cream
1 tablespoon, plus 1 teaspoon sugar, divided
2 cups cooked pinto or kidney beans, rinsed and drained
1 (28-ounce) can whole tomatoes with juice
½ cup dehydrated onion
1 teaspoon dried garlic powder
¼ cup dried peaches, cut into ¼" dice
¼ cup dried apricots, cut into ¼" dice
2 tablespoons raisins
½ teaspoon thyme
1 (4") cinnamon stick
Pinch ground allspice
Pinch ground cloves
Pinch ground nutmeg
Pinch cider vinegar
¼ cup fresh pomegranate seeds

......................................................................................................

**1.** Preheat oven to 350°F.

**2.** Pre-cook peppers: Wash poblanos, pat dry, and rub all over with oil. Sprinkle with ¼ teaspoon salt. Place in a small baking dish, cover dish tightly with foil, and bake until peppers are soft, about 50–60 minutes. Remove foil and set peppers aside.

**3.** Make sauce: Place walnuts, half-and-half, 1 tablespoon sugar, and ¼ teaspoon salt into the bowl of a blender or food processor and blend until smooth, about 5 minutes. Adjust salt to taste. If sauce is too thick, add water by the tablespoon until it reaches desired consistency. Transfer sauce to a storage container and refrigerate until ready to use.

# Stuffed Green Chilies with Pinto Beans and Dried Fruit (continued)

**4.** Make filling: Place pintos, tomatoes, onion, garlic, dried fruit, thyme, cinnamon, allspice, cloves, nutmeg, vinegar, and remaining 1 teaspoon sugar into a large heavy pot. Bring to a boil over medium heat, and then reduce heat to low and simmer 30 minutes. Remove cinnamon stick and mash coarsely with potato masher. Season to taste with remaining ½ teaspoon salt.

**5.** Assemble dish: Cut each poblano lengthwise on one side, leaving ¼" near the stem and ¼" at the tip. Remove seeds, leaving stem intact. Stuff each poblano with ¼ of the bean mixture. Transfer stuffed peppers to baking dish, cover with foil, and bake until heated through, 10–15 minutes.

**6.** To serve, transfer each poblano to a plate, top with ¼ of the walnut sauce, and sprinkle with 1 tablespoon pomegranate seeds.

# Whipped Sweet Potatoes with Toasted Dried Coconut

**Makes 4 servings.**

*Skip the brown sugar, pecans, and marshmallows the next time you're serving sweet potatoes. Instead, you can get all the same flavors—toastiness and sweetness—with the addition of toasted coconut. The whipped potatoes also make an excellent filling for ravioli or between the layers of noodles in a lasagna.*

## Ingredients

½ cup dried coconut

1 teaspoon salt, divided

1 pound sweet potatoes, scrubbed, peeled, and cut into 1" cubes

2 tablespoons unsalted butter

¼ cup milk

¼ cup pineapple juice (may substitute orange juice)

½ teaspoon dried ginger powder

Pinch cayenne pepper

**1.** Place dried coconut in a medium skillet over medium heat and cook, stirring constantly, until golden brown, about 5 minutes. Transfer coconut immediately to a plate and set aside to cool.

**2.** Bring a large pot of water to a boil over high heat. When boiling, add ½ teaspoon of salt and sweet potato cubes. Boil, uncovered, until potatoes are tender, about 20 minutes. Drain and transfer to the bowl of a food processor or blender.

**3.** Add remaining ingredients and process until smooth.

**4.** Serve sweet potatoes topped with toasted coconut.

# CHAPTER 12
# Sweets

The perfect ending to any meal is a sweet treat. These desserts are destined to be the sweetest treat—they take the freshest fruits, dried at their peak of flavor, and add in traditional favorites, such as ice cream and chocolate.

# Baked Apples

**Makes 4 servings.**

*A simple and sweet end to any meal, baked apples will soon become a staple in your home once you start dehydrating fruits. They are a great way to experiment with different fruits. You can make mainstream baked apples with dried raisins, a summer version with dried berries, or an island version with dried tropical fruits. Feel free to mix up the nuts you use in this recipe—while pecans go nicely with dried fall fruits, macadamias work well with kiwi, pineapple, coconut, and mango.*

## Ingredients

4 firm baking apples, such as gala, Granny Smith, or honeycrisp

¼ cup mixed dried fruit, cut into raisin-sized pieces

3 tablespoons brown sugar

3 tablespoons pecans or walnuts, chopped

2 tablespoons maple syrup

¼ cup water

2 tablespoons unsalted butter, divided into 4 pieces

1 (3"–4") cinnamon stick

2 whole cloves

1. Preheat oven to 350°F.
2. Wash apples. Using a melon baller, core apples from the top to roughly ½" from the bottom, leaving the rest of the apple intact. Set apples into a medium baking dish.
3. Mix dried fruit, brown sugar, and nuts together in a small bowl. Fill the cavity in each apple with ¼ of the dried fruit mixture, pressing slightly to pack in filling.
4. Drizzle maple syrup over apples and onto bottom of pan. Pour water around apples into bottom of pan.
5. Place ½ tablespoon of butter on top of the filling in each apple. Add cinnamon and cloves to liquid around apples. Cover dish tightly with foil and bake until apples are soft, about 35–45 minutes.
6. Remove cinnamon and cloves and discard. Remove apples carefully with a slotted spoon and serve with some of the sauce. If desired, first transfer sauce to a pan and boil until the thickness of maple syrup, about 5 minutes.

# Black Forest Brownies

**Makes 16 servings.**

*These dense, fudgy brownies bring together delicious dried cherries and dark chocolate to evoke the flavors of black forest cake, the traditional German dessert. Served with a dollop of whipped cream, they are a welcome end to any fabulous meal or even a hectic workday.*

## Ingredients

½ cup dried cherries

8 ounces bittersweet chocolate (cacao content should be 60% or higher)

8 tablespoons unsalted butter

3 eggs

1 cup sugar

1 teaspoon vanilla extract

1 tablespoon kirsch (optional)

1 cup flour

1 cup whipping cream, whipped to soft peaks with ¼ cup sugar and 1 teaspoon vanilla extract, or 1 canister prepared whipped cream

1. Cover dried cherries with hot water and soak until softened, about 20 minutes.
2. Preheat oven to 350°F.
3. Grease and flour an 8" × 9" square baking pan.
4. Chop chocolate into ½" pieces. Cut butter into pats. Combine in a heatproof medium bowl.
5. Place a pan of water over high heat and bring to a boil. Reduce heat to a simmer and place bowl with chocolate and butter into pan of water, taking care not to splash any water into the bowl. Melt together chocolate and butter, stirring constantly, until completely melted, about 7 minutes. Remove from pan of water and set aside.
6. Combine eggs, sugar, vanilla, and kirsch. Slowly add melted chocolate, stirring constantly.
7. Drain cherries. Add cherries and flour to chocolate mixture. Pour into prepared pan, spreading batter into an even layer.
8. Bake until toothpick inserted into the center comes out clean, 30–40 minutes. Transfer pan to a rack and allow to cool completely.
9. Cut brownies into squares and serve with whipped cream.

### Save Your Hands

One of the best things about summer is cherries. Buy some just for drying. Removing the pits can be a chore so invest in an inexpensive cherry pitter. And pitting them can stain your hands, so it's best to wear a pair of rubber gloves while you're working with them, or better yet disposable ones.

# Caramel Apple Bread Pudding

**Makes 8 servings.**

*This is a great dessert to make the morning of a dinner party and then bake in the oven when you're dining. A take on caramel apples, you mix dehydrated apples with caramel sauce and top with chopped salted peanuts. The flavor combination brings salted caramel—as well as childhood after-school treats—firmly to mind.*

## Ingredients

For the bread pudding:
8 large eggs
2 cups whole milk
2 cups half-and-half
1 cup sugar
1 teaspoon vanilla
12 thick slices stale bread, crusts trimmed, cut into cubes
¾ cup dried apples

For the topping:
1 cup sugar
¼ cup water
4 tablespoons butter, cut into squares
½ cup heavy cream
1 teaspoon vanilla extract
½ cup Spanish peanuts, roughly chopped, optional

**1.** Butter a 13" × 9" × 2" glass baking dish.

**2.** In a large bowl, beat together eggs, milk, half-and-half, sugar, and vanilla until well blended.

**3.** Add bread cubes and apples and mix well. Transfer to prepared baking dish, pushing bread into egg mixture. Wrap tightly with plastic wrap. Refrigerate 1 hour or more (up to 10 hours).

**4.** When ready to bake bread pudding, preheat oven to 325°F. Unwrap bread pudding. Bake until golden and center is set, about 45 minutes. When finished baking, let it rest 10 minutes.

**5.** While bread pudding bakes, make caramel sauce. Mix sugar and water together in a heavy saucepan. Cook over medium-high heat, stirring constantly, until sugar water turns a golden brown, about 5 minutes. Remove from heat, and whisk in butter until melted and completely absorbed. While whisking, slowly add cream and vanilla until completely absorbed.

**6.** To serve, cut bread pudding into 3" × 3" squares. Pour caramel sauce over each piece and sprinkle with peanuts, if using.

# Chocolate-Dipped Fruits

**Makes 8 servings.**

*While store-bought dried fruits come in set shapes, you're better able to control the size and shape of fruit you dry at home. By dipping dried fruits into chocolate, you can show off your handiwork. The secret to this recipe is to melt most of the chocolate and then take it off the heat and stir in the remaining chocolate. That renders exceptionally glossy chocolate that has the characteristic "crack" when you bite into it. Feel free to adorn your chocolate-dipped fruits with toasted dried coconut, crystallized ginger, or chopped, toasted nuts.*

## Ingredients

2 cups mixed dried fruits

Toothpicks

4 ounces dark, semi-sweet, milk, or white chocolate, finely chopped

........................................................................................

**1.** Skewer each piece of dried fruit with a toothpick. Line a baking sheet with foil, wax paper, or parchment paper.

**2.** Bring a large skillet of water to boil over high heat. Reduce heat and keep water at a simmer. Place ¾ of chocolate into a heatproof bowl and place bowl into skillet. Melt chocolate, stirring constantly. When chocolate is completely melted, remove from heat. Immediately stir in reserved chocolate and stir until melted.

**3.** Dip each piece of fruit into chocolate, swirling to coat. Transfer coated fruit to prepared baking sheet.

**4.** Keep dipped fruit at room temperature until set, about 1 hour. Serve or transfer to an airtight container. Store in a cool, dark place, but do not store in the refrigerator.

# Citrus-Kissed Shortbread

**Makes 8 servings.**

*Traditional Scottish shortbread is a buttery delight that welcomes other subtle flavors. One nice way to augment shortbread is with a bit of citrus, which cuts the richness. You'll enjoy noticing the variations that different types of citrus bring to your shortbread—from the freshness of lemon to the bitter touch of grapefruit.*

## Ingredients

½ cup sugar, divided

1 cup flour

2 tablespoons cornstarch

¼ teaspoon salt

½ teaspoon dried citrus (lemon, lime, orange), cut into fine dice

1 stick cold unsalted butter, cut into 1-tablespoon pats

**1.** Preheat oven to 425°F. Butter and flour a 9" springform pan.

**2.** Remove 1 tablespoon sugar from ½ cup and set aside. Sift remaining sugar, flour, cornstarch, and salt together into a mixing bowl. Stir in citrus. Work butter into flour mixture using a pastry cutter until the mixture resembles sand. Pour mixture into an even layer in springform pan and press down firmly to create an even layer of dough.

**3.** Place in oven and drop temperature to 300°F. Bake until just set, but not brown, about 15–20 minutes. Remove pan from oven and cut shortbread halfway through into pieces. (This way it will break easily when fully baked.) Return to oven and bake until lightly browned, about 25–30 minutes longer.

**4.** Remove from oven. Remove outer springform and sprinkle top of shortbread with remaining sugar. Allow to rest until cool enough to handle, about 15 minutes. Transfer shortbread to a cutting board and cut into pieces. Transfer pieces to a wire rack and allow to cool 2–4 hours. Serve or store in an airtight container.

# Coconut and Crystallized Ginger Ice Cream

**Makes 8 servings.**

*This ice cream is a cool dessert that brings out the flavors found in warm climates—coconut and ginger. If you don't have an ice cream maker, you can make the cream base and freeze it in a baking dish. When firm, whip it in your food processor, then stir in the coconut and ginger.*

## Ingredients

½ cup dried coconut

¼ cup dried sliced ginger

1 cup water

1⅓ cups sugar, divided

2 cups whole milk

6 egg yolks

1 cup heavy cream

1 tablespoon coconut extract

1. Heat a large stainless steel or cast iron skillet over medium heat. Add dried coconut and toast, stirring constantly, until coconut is golden brown, about 7 minutes. Immediately transfer coconut to a plate to cool.

2. Place ginger in a wire mesh strainer and rinse under cold running water. Place in a small bowl and cover with hot water. Soak until softened, about 20 minutes. Drain.

3. Place softened ginger into a small saucepan with water and ⅔ cup sugar. Bring to a boil over high heat. Reduce heat and simmer 30 minutes. Remove ginger from syrup, reserving syrup for another use, and allow ginger to cool on a wire rack until completely cooled, about 30 minutes. Coarsely chop ginger.

4. Place milk in a small saucepan. Bring to a boil and remove from heat.

5. Whisk together remaining sugar and egg yolks until very thick and pale yellow.

6. While whisking the egg mixture, slowly add half of hot milk. Return mixture to the saucepan with the remaining milk, and cook over medium heat, stirring constantly until mixture thickens, about 5–7 minutes.

7. Strain mixture through a wire mesh strainer into a bowl that's set over a second bowl filled with ice water. Add cream and coconut extract and stir the mixture until it's at room temperature, about 10 minutes. Cover and refrigerate for 2 hours.

8. Transfer to an ice cream maker and freeze according to the manufacturer's instructions. When ice cream is finished processing, add toasted coconut and crystallized ginger. Stir and serve.

### No Ice Cream Maker?

Don't worry if you want to try this recipe but don't own an ice cream maker or food processor. Simply put all the ingredients in a zipper bag and place it on its side in the freezer. Check it every hour and squeeze the ingredients as they freeze.

# Cranberry Sauce Bars with Dried Mixed Berries

**Makes 32 (1" × 2") bars.**

*Although originally developed as a way to use leftover cranberry sauce, you'll find these bars are a reason to make cranberry sauce in the first place. The combination of fresh berries with dried berries accentuates the sweet-tart nature of the cranberries themselves.*

## Ingredients

3 cups fresh cranberries

1½ cups water

1 cup sugar

2–3 slices dried orange or tangerine, optional

1½ cups dried mixed berries

1¼ cups oats

2 cups flour

¾ cup brown sugar, packed

½ teaspoon ground cinnamon

¼ teaspoon ground allspice

½ teaspoon baking powder

½ teaspoon baking soda

½ teaspoon salt

1½ sticks cold, unsalted butter, cut into 1-tablespoon pats

2 tablespoons unsalted butter, melted

**1.** Place fresh cranberries, water, sugar, and orange slices (if using) into a medium saucepan. Bring to a boil over high heat. Reduce heat and simmer, stirring occasionally, until all cranberries have "popped" and softened, about 20 minutes. Remove from heat and remove orange slices, if using. Stir in dried berries and chill until set, about 1 hour.

**2.** Preheat oven to 350°F. Line an 8" × 8" baking pan with foil. Spray foil with pan spray or brush with oil.

**3.** Place oats, flour, brown sugar, cinnamon, allspice, baking powder, baking soda, and salt in a large bowl. Stir to combine. Using your hands or a pastry cutter, add 1½ sticks chilled butter until well combined and the texture of sand.

**4.** Press half of oat mixture firmly into bottom of pan.

**5.** Bake until golden, about 20 minutes. Remove from oven and spread with cranberry sauce in an even layer. Mix remaining mixture with melted butter and sprinkle over cranberry sauce.

**6.** Bake until set, about 45 minutes. Transfer to a wire rack to cool.

**7.** Cool to room temperature. Cut into 1" × 2" bars and serve.

# Lavender Crème Brûlée

**Makes 8 servings.**

*With its crunchy caramelized sugar topping and creamy middle, crème brûlée delights most diners. Although fruit and chocolate are welcome additions to this classic dessert, so are dried herbs. In this recipe, you can pair dried lavender with egg and cream for a lightly floral taste. For broader palates, experiment with other dried herbs such as rosemary or thyme.*

## Ingredients

3 cups heavy cream

1 teaspoon dried lavender flowers

1 vanilla bean, split and scraped

1¼ cups sugar, divided

6 egg yolks

......................................................................................................

**1.** Preheat oven to 325°F. Line a roasting pan with a double layer of newspaper. Arrange eight 6- to 8-ounce ramekins or custard cups in roasting pan.

**2.** Place cream, lavender, and vanilla in a heavy small saucepan. Bring to a boil over medium heat. Immediately remove from heat, cover, and allow to steep 20 minutes.

**3.** Beat ¾ cup sugar and yolks in large bowl until pale yellow and thick, about 3–4 minutes. Strain cream through a wire mesh strainer, discarding solids. Slowly beat strained cream into egg mixture and immediately pour even amounts into ramekins. Pour hot water into roasting pan until water is halfway up sides of ramekins.

**4.** Bake until set in center, about 50 minutes. Remove ramekins from roasting pan and allow to cool to room temperature, about 1 hour. Refrigerate until completely chilled, 2–4 hours.

**5.** To serve, preheat broiler. Place ramekins on a baking sheet (if using a nonstick pan, line pan with foil to prevent damage to the nonstick coating). Sprinkle 1 tablespoon sugar evenly across the surface of each custard.

**6.** Place under broiler and broil until tops are dark golden brown, about 2 minutes. Serve.

......................................................................................................

### Easy to Grow

Did you know there are several varieties of lavender, such as English, French, and Spanish sage, and all are easy to grow? They don't need much attention, are fairly drought resistant, and spread and multiply without much help. Lavender's also perfect for drying and not only can be used in cooking but can be part of crafts as well, such as fragrance sachets for your closet.

......................................................................................................

# Marbled Banana and Dark Chocolate Fruit Leather

**Makes 8 servings.**

*Fruit leather may be a lunchbox staple. However, marbled banana and dark chocolate fruit leather is a reason to look forward to lunch. Chewy and chocolatey, this dessert seems decadent, but it isn't. Because it's based on bananas and dark chocolate, you don't have to worry about its impact on your waistline.*

## Ingredients

4 bananas

1 teaspoon fresh lemon juice

4 ounces dark (60% cacao or more) chocolate, finely chopped

........................................................................................

**1.** Line a food dehydrator rack with foil, wax paper, or parchment paper. Spray with pan spray.

**2.** Peel bananas and place bananas and lemon juice in the bowl of a blender or food processor. Blend until smooth. Remove half of mixture and set aside.

**3.** Place chocolate into a microwave-safe bowl. Cook in the microwave on medium-high, stirring every 15–20 seconds, checking to see whether chocolate is completely melted, about 4–6 minutes, depending upon the power of your microwave. Add ¼ melted chocolate to blender and purée. Repeat with remaining chocolate, adding chocolate a little bit at a time. Once all chocolate is incorporated, purée mixture until smooth.

**4.** Pour reserved banana mixture and chocolate mixture in alternating 1" sections onto tray.

**5.** Using a wooden spoon or offset spatula, swirl the mixtures into one another, creating a marble pattern.

**6.** Dehydrate at 130°F until set and dry to the touch, 8–10 hours.

**7.** Remove from dehydrator and allow to come to room temperature, about 30 minutes. Peel from backing, cut into 2" × 4" pieces, and store in an airtight container.

........................................................................................

### Elvis Would Have Loved It

If you're not worried about counting calories and you want to turn this into a real treat, try adding 2 tablespoons peanut butter to the banana mixture. It adds more richness and texture and pairs beautifully with the chocolate element of this dessert.

........................................................................................

# Spiced Chili Pepper Hot Chocolate

**Makes 4 servings.**

*This hot chocolate was inspired by the chocolate beverages first served in Central and South America, which contained spices and chili peppers. The dark chocolate blends seamlessly with dried chilies, cinnamon, and citrus, making for an intoxicating hot beverage. If you don't have three people to share your hot cocoa with, not to worry—you can refrigerate leftover hot chocolate and reheat it to enjoy a different day.*

## Ingredients

3 cups whole or 2% milk

1 small or ½ large dried chili pepper, left in a single piece

3 cinnamon sticks

3 star anise

1 slice dried ginger

1 slice dried orange or tangerine

6 ounces dark chocolate, finely chopped

½ teaspoon vanilla

Pinch salt

**1.** Place milk, pepper, cinnamon, anise, ginger, and orange into a saucepot. Bring to a boil over high heat. Immediately remove from heat, cover, and steep 30 minutes. Strain milk, discarding solids.

**2.** Bring milk to a boil again, and immediately remove from heat. Whisk in chocolate, vanilla, and salt. When well combined, serve.

# Sunshine Cake with Dried Pineapple

**Makes 8–12 servings.**

*This cake features dehydrated citrus powder with the sweetness of dried pineapple. Pay special attention to using a clean bowl to whip the egg whites. A quick rinse in vinegar will remove any oils from the bowl that might inhibit stiff peaks from forming.*

## Ingredients

½ tablespoon unsalted butter

1 tablespoon all-purpose flour

1 tablespoon neutral vinegar, such as distilled white, rice, or white wine vinegar

6 eggs

1 cup cake flour

¼ teaspoon baking powder

¼ teaspoon salt

1½ cups sugar, divided three ways

1½ teaspoons vanilla extract, divided

1 slice dehydrated lemon, orange, or tangerine, powdered

¾ teaspoon cream of tartar

1½ cups whipping cream

½ cup dried pineapple

......................................................................................................

**1.** Preheat oven to 350°F. Butter and flour two 9" or 10" cake pans with all-purpose flour.

**2.** Prepare a mixing bowl to whip egg whites: Clean a large mixing bowl and dry thoroughly. Pour vinegar into bowl and swirl to coat inside. Pour excess vinegar out. Separate eggs, placing whites into the bowl with vinegar and yolks into another large bowl.

**3.** Sift together cake flour, baking powder, and salt. Set aside.

**4.** Add ⅔ cup sugar to egg yolks. Beat on high speed until light yellow and thick, about 3 minutes. Add 1 teaspoon vanilla extract and powdered citrus.

**5.** Fold flour mixture into egg yolk mixture. Set aside.

**6.** Using clean beaters, beat egg whites and cream of tartar to soft peaks. Add ⅓ cup sugar and beat to stiff peaks.

**7.** Fold ½ cup of beaten egg whites into egg yolk mixture. When fully incorporated, fold in remaining whites. Divide batter evenly among prepared cake pans. Smooth tops of each cake with an offset spatula.

**8.** Bake cakes until a toothpick comes out clean when inserted into the center of each cake, about 20–25 minutes.

# Sunshine Cake with Dried Pineapple (continued)

**9.** Cool cakes on wire rack 10 minutes. Remove cakes from pans and allow to cool completely on wire racks, about 1 hour.

**10.** Whip cream to soft peaks, slowly add remaining ½ cup sugar and remaining ½ teaspoon vanilla extract, and continue whipping 1 minute.

**11.** Spread whipped cream onto one cake in an even layer. Sprinkle with dried pineapple. Place second cake on top, pressing gently to get top cake to adhere. Cut into slices and serve.

# Untraditional Trifle

**Makes 8 servings.**

*While a traditional British trifle combines a sponge cake, custard, jam, and sherry, this recipe opts for a simpler no-cook version. Perfect for making when you have impromptu guests, simply cube whatever cake you have on hand, rehydrate berries and apricots (or any fruit, for that matter) in port, and layer with whipped cream. It is stunning in a large clear glass bowl or made into individual servings in balloon wine glasses.*

## Ingredients

1 cup dried apricots, nectarines, or peaches, or a mixture, chopped into ¼" dice

1 cup dried blackberries, blueberries, cherries, or strawberries, or a mixture

2 cups ruby port

3 cups whipping cream

1 cup sugar

1 teaspoon vanilla extract

1 pound cake or angel food cake, cut into ½" cubes

¼ cup chopped toasted pecans or toasted coconut

........................................................................................................

**1.** Place fruit in a wire mesh strainer and rinse under cold running water. Transfer to a medium bowl.

**2.** Bring port to a boil and pour over fruit. Allow to steep until fruit softens, about 20 minutes. Strain fruit and place port in a small saucepan over medium heat. Bring to a boil and cook until reduced by half, about 5 minutes.

**3.** Whip cream to soft peaks, slowly add sugar and vanilla extract, and continue whipping 1 minute.

**4.** Place half of cake cubes into a large, clear bowl. Top with half of reduced port, half of rehydrated fruit, and half of whipped cream. Repeat with remaining cake, port, fruit, and whipped cream. Sprinkle with toasted pecans and serve.

# Vanilla Bean Gelato with Dried Strawberries

**Makes 8 servings.**

*Your own homemade vanilla ice cream is an indulgent treat that gets an upgrade from orange-kissed dried strawberries. If you don't have an ice cream maker, or would like a shortcut for this recipe, buy high quality vanilla ice cream. Prepare the strawberries as directed in the recipe. Soften the ice cream for 5 minutes at room temperature and stir in the strained strawberries.*

## Ingredients

¼ cup dried strawberries

½ cup triple sec

2 cups whole milk

1 vanilla bean, split lengthwise and scraped, or
   1 teaspoon vanilla extract

⅔ cup sugar

6 egg yolks

1 cup heavy cream

........................................................................................

**1.** Cut strawberries into ¼" pieces. Rinse dried strawberries. Place into a glass jar and cover with triple sec. Allow to soften at room temperature for 1 or more hours.

**2.** If using vanilla extract, skip to the next step. If using a vanilla bean, combine milk, vanilla bean, and vanilla seeds in a medium saucepan. Bring to a simmer, then remove from heat, cover, and let steep 20 minutes.

**3.** Whisk together sugar and egg yolks until very thick and pale yellow.

**4.** Remove vanilla bean (if using) from milk or stir vanilla extract into milk and bring back to a simmer. While whisking the egg mixture, slowly add half of hot milk. Return mixture to the saucepan with the remaining milk, and cook over medium heat, stirring constantly, until mixture thickens, about 5–7 minutes.

**5.** Strain mixture through a wire mesh strainer into a bowl that's set over a second bowl filled with ice water. Add cream and stir the mixture until it's room temperature, about 10 minutes. Cover and refrigerate for 2 hours.

**6.** Transfer to an ice cream maker and freeze according to the manufacturer's instructions. When gelato is finished processing, drain strawberries, reserving triple sec for another use. Add strawberries to gelato and serve.

........................................................................................

### Whip Up Another Dessert

Don't worry if you're wondering what you can do with the leftover egg whites after you've made this dish. Try a homemade lemon or key lime meringue pie. Or you can use them with another dried goodie, pineapple, and make some macaroons with diced dried pineapple as an ingredient.

........................................................................................

# STANDARD U.S./
# METRIC MEASUREMENT CONVERSIONS

## VOLUME CONVERSIONS

| U.S. Volume Measure | Metric Equivalent |
| --- | --- |
| ⅛ teaspoon | 0.5 milliliters |
| ¼ teaspoon | 1 milliliters |
| ½ teaspoon | 2 milliliters |
| 1 teaspoon | 5 milliliters |
| ½ tablespoon | 7 milliliters |
| 1 tablespoon (3 teaspoons) | 15 milliliters |
| 2 tablespoons (1 fluid ounce) | 30 milliliters |
| ¼ cup (4 tablespoons) | 60 milliliters |
| ⅓ cup | 90 milliliters |
| ½ cup (4 fluid ounces) | 125 milliliters |
| ⅔ cup | 160 milliliters |
| ¾ cup (6 fluid ounces) | 180 milliliters |
| 1 cup (16 tablespoons) | 250 milliliters |
| 1 pint (2 cups) | 500 milliliters |
| 1 quart (4 cups) | 1 liter (about) |

## WEIGHT CONVERSIONS

| U.S. Weight Measure | Metric Equivalent |
| --- | --- |
| ½ ounce | 15 grams |
| 1 ounce | 30 grams |
| 2 ounces | 60 grams |
| 3 ounces | 85 grams |
| ¼ pound (4 ounces) | 115 grams |
| ½ pound (8 ounces) | 225 grams |
| ¾ pound (12 ounces) | 340 grams |
| 1 pound (16 ounces) | 454 grams |

## OVEN TEMPERATURE CONVERSIONS

| Degrees Fahrenheit | Degrees Celsius |
| --- | --- |
| 200 degrees F | 95 degrees C |
| 250 degrees F | 120 degrees C |
| 275 degrees F | 135 degrees C |
| 300 degrees F | 150 degrees C |
| 325 degrees F | 160 degrees C |
| 350 degrees F | 180 degrees C |
| 375 degrees F | 190 degrees C |
| 400 degrees F | 205 degrees C |
| 425 degrees F | 220 degrees C |
| 450 degrees F | 230 degrees C |

## BAKING PAN SIZES

| U.S. | Metric |
| --- | --- |
| 8 × 1½ inch round baking pan | 20 × 4 cm cake tin |
| 9 × 1½ inch round baking pan | 23 × 3.5 cm cake tin |
| 11 × 7 × 1½ inch baking pan | 28 × 18 × 4 cm baking tin |
| 13 × 9 × 2 inch baking pan | 30 × 20 × 5 cm baking tin |
| 2 quart rectangular baking dish | 30 × 20 × 3 cm baking tin |
| 15 × 10 × 2 inch baking pan | 30 × 25 × 2 cm baking tin (Swiss roll tin) |
| 9 inch pie plate | 22 × 4 or 23 × 4 cm pie plate |
| 7 or 8 inch springform pan | 18 or 20 cm springform or loose bottom cake tin |
| 9 × 5 × 3 inch loaf pan | 23 × 13 × 7 cm or 2 lb narrow loaf or pate tin |
| 1½ quart casserole | 1.5 liter casserole |
| 2 quart casserole | 2 liter casserole |

# Index

# About the Authors

**Susan Palmquist** is a freelance writer and bestselling author of forty books. Her articles have appeared in both the United States and UK in such publications as *Arthritis Today*, *Health*, *My Weekly*, and *Natural Living*, and on Lifetime TV. She's written two food-related columns and been food editor for an online health community. Prior to her writing career she worked in PR and was a book publicist for three years. Food-related topics have always been her passion. She took cooking classes for four years, taught cooking lessons, and is currently a member of the Foodies UK network. She's now working on her next cookbook. When she's not writing, she's teaching workshops and tutoring aspiring writers. Born and raised in London, England, she currently resides in the Midwest. Find out more about Susan and her work at *www.susanpalmquist.com*.

**Jill Houk** honed her culinary skills as a professional catering chef and cooking instructor, but even more than cooking, she loves developing new products and recipes for consumers. Although she originally pursued a career in information technology consulting, she later followed her dream of becoming a chef. She adeptly combines these two disciplines into culinary consulting—mixing the research and project-management skills she practiced in information technology with her knowledge of flavors, cooking techniques, and consumer dining trends that she learned as a chef. This dynamic combination enables Chef Houk to create food-related strategies and tactics that promote and sell products for clients such as Ajinomoto, Applegate Farms, Driscoll's Berries, Sara Lee, and World Kitchen. She has appeared on national television on *Good Morning America*, on Lifetime Television, and on the Cooking Channel. She is also co-host of *Kitchen Cookoff* on delish.com.